General Editor: James Gibson

Published

JANE AUSTEN	*Emma*
	Pride and Prejudice Raymond Wilson
	Mansfield Park Richard Wirdnam
ROBERT BOLT	*A Man for all Seasons* Leonard Smith
EMILY BRONTË	*Wuthering Heights* Hilda D. Spear
GEOFFREY CHAUCER	*The Miller's Tale* Michael Alexander
	The Prologue to the Canterbury Tales Nigel Thomas and Richard Swan
CHARLES DICKENS	*Bleak House* Dennis Butts
	Great Expectations Dennis Butts
	Hard Times Norman Page
GEORGE ELIOT	*Middlemarch* Graham Handley
	Silas Marner Graham Handley
	The Mill on the Floss Helen Wheeler
E.M. FORSTER	*A Passage to India* Hilda D. Spear
THE METAPHYSICAL POETS	Joan van Emden
WILLIAM GOLDING	*The Spire* Rosemary Sumner
	Lord of the Flies Raymond Wilson
OLIVER GOLDSMITH	*She Stoops to Conquer* Paul Ranger
THOMAS HARDY	*The Mayor of Casterbridge* Ray Evans
	Tess of the D'Urbervilles James Gibson
	Far from the Madding Crowd Colin Temblett-Wood
PHILIP LARKIN	*The Less Deceived and The Whitsun Wedding* Andrew Swarbrick
D.H. LAWRENCE	*Sons and Lovers* Ronald Draper
CHRISTOPHER MARLOWE	*Doctor Faustus* David A. Male
THOMAS MIDDLETON and WILLIAM ROWLEY	*The Changeling* Tony Bromham
ARTHUR MILLER	*The Crucible* Leonard Smith
GEORGE ORWELL	*Animal Farm* Jean Armstrong
WILLIAM SHAKESPEARE	*Hamlet* Jean Brooks
	King Lear Francis Casey
	The Winter's Tale Diana Devlin
	Julius Caesar David Elloway
	Macbeth David Elloway
	Measure for Measure Mark Lilly
	A Midsummer Night's Dream Kenneth Pickering

	Henry IV Part I Helen Morris
	Romeo and Juliet Helen Morris
	The Tempest Kenneth Pickering
GEORGE BERNARD SHAW	*St Joan* Leonèe Ormond
RICHARD SHERIDAN	*The School for Scandal* Paul Ranger
	The Rivals Jeremy Rowe
JOHN WEBSTER	*The White Devil and The Duchess of Malfi* David A. Male

Forthcoming

JANE AUSTEN	*Sense and Sensibility* Judy Simons
SAMUEL BECKETT	*Waiting for Godot* Jennifer Birkett
WILLIAM BLAKE	*Songs of Innocence and Songs of Experience* Alan Tomlinson
GEOFFREY CHAUCER	*The Pardoner's Tale* Geoff Lester
	The Wife of Bath's Tale Nicholas Marsh
	The Knight's Tale Anne Samson
T.S. ELIOT	*Murder in the Cathedral* Paul Lapworth
HENRY FIELDING	*Joseph Andrews* Trevor Johnson
E.M. FORSTER	*Howard's End* Ian Milligan
GERARD MANLEY HOPKINS	*Selected Poems* R. Watt
BEN JONSON	*Volpone* Michael Stout
JOHN KEATS	*Selected Poems* John Garrett
HARPER LEE	*To Kill a Mockingbird* Jean Armstrong
ARTHUR MILLER	*Death of a Salesman* Peter Spalding
WILLIAM SHAKESPEARE	*Richard II* Charles Barber
	Othello Christopher Beddowes
	Henry V Peter Davison
	As You Like It Kiernan Ryan
	Twelfth Night Edward Leeson
ALFRED TENNYSON	*In Memoriam* Richard Gill

Further titles are in preparation

MACMILLAN MASTER GUIDES
THE SPIRE
BY WILLIAM GOLDING

ROSEMARY SUMNER

MACMILLAN

First edition 1986

Published by
MACMILLAN EDUCATION LTD
Houndmills, Basingstoke, Hampshire RG21 2XS
and London
Companies and representatives
throughout the world

Typeset by
TecSet, Sutton, Surrey

Printed in Hong Kong

British Library Cataloguing in Publication Data
Sumner, Rosemary
The spire by William Golding. — (Macmillan
master guides)
1. 1. Golding, William. Spire
I. Title   II. Golding, William
823'914   PR6013.035S6
ISBN 0-333-39774-6
ISBN 0-333-39775-4 Pbk export

CONTENTS

GENERAL EDITOR'S PREFACE

The aim of the Macmillan Master Guides is to help you to appreciate the book you are studying by providing information about it and by suggesting ways of reading and thinking about it which will lead to a fuller understanding. The section on the writer's life and background has been designed to illustrate those aspects of the writer's life which have influenced the work, and to place it in its personal and literary context. The summaries and critical commentary are of special importance in that each brief summary of the action is followed by an examination of the significant critical points. The space which might have been given to repetitive explanatory notes has been devoted to a detailed analysis of the kind of passage which might confront you in an examination. Literary criticism is concerned with both the broader aspects of the work being studied and with its detail. The ideas which meet us in reading a great work of literature, and their relevance to us today, are an essential part of our study, and our Guides look at the thought of their subject in some detail. But just as essential is the craft with which the writer has constructed his work of art, and this may be considered under several technical headings – characterisation, language, style and stagecraft, for example.

The authors of these Guides are all teachers and writers of wide experience, and they have chosen to write about books they admire and know well in the belief that they can communicate their admiration to you. But you yourself must read and know intimately the book you are studying. No one can do that for you. You should see this book as a lamp-post. Use it to shed light, not to lean against. If you know your text and know what it is saying about life, and how it says it, then you will enjoy it, and there is no better way of passing an examination in literature.

JAMES GIBSON

ACKNOWLEDGEMENTS

I am indebted to those colleagues and students with whom I have discussed Golding over the years, and especially to J. Burke; J. Clough; S. Dobson; N. Gamble; J. Greig; L. Matthews; W. Minster; S. Richards; P. Ridge, C. Smith and L. Tenn who allowed me to record their seminars and use them in any way I chose. Nevertheless, the characters in Chapter 3 are purely fictitious and bear no relation to any student I have known.

The author and publishers wish to thank Faber and Faber Ltd. who have kindly given permission for use of extracts from *The Spire* by William Golding.

Cover illustration: A detail from *Salisbury Cathedral from the* Meadows by John Constable, courtesy of the Bridgeman Art Library.

'It is our business to describe the indescribable.'

WILLIAM GOLDING

1 WILLIAM GOLDING: LIFE AND BACKGROUND

1.1   AUTOBIOGRAPHY

It would be possible to construct a fragmentary autobiography out of William Golding's non-fiction writing. It would start with 'Billy the Kid' (*The Hot Gates*, 159-65), an account of his first pugnacious days at school; woven into this essay are hints of the future novelist – Billy's aggressiveness is mixed with sensitivity; his imagination is obsessed with words. Next would come 'Egypt from my Inside' (*The Hot Gates* 71-82) which describes visits he made at the age of 8 or 9 to the Egyptian section of a museum, where he recognised in the mummies something akin to 'my own mournful staring into the darkness, my own savage grasp on life'. 'The Ladder and the Tree' seems to deal with the following few years. Again, he dwells on his vivid consciousness of darkness and mysteriousness. He stresses his fears about the ancient cellar under his family's fourteenth-century house and about the bodies in the adjoining churchyard, and his awareness that climbing 'rung after factual rung' of the ladder of rationality will still leave the darkness 'all around, inexplicable, unexorcised, haunted'. In spite of this, he accepted his parents' desire for him to climb that ladder. There are other glimpses of his childhood scattered through his essays – references to his first visits to Salisbury Cathedral clinging to his mother's hand ('An Affection for Cathedrals', *A Moving Target*, 14), to lessons at his infant school ('My First Book', *A Moving Target*, 147).

Similarly, his later life tends to be revealed in the essays by passing references to his own experiences. There is a brief, mocking, comment on his part as a naval officer on D-Day in 'The English Channel' (*The Hot Gates*, 42); *Pincher Martin* uses knowledge acquired at that time much more fully than the essay. Although being in the wartime navy clearly had a great impact on Golding, even more profound was the effect of the knowledge, shared by everyone since the war, of the concentration camps and the gas-chambers. As he explains in 'Fable' (*The Hot Gates*, 85-101), this led him to see man as diseased, essentially evil, and he felt that it was only through recognising this that society could improve. *Lord of the Flies* illustrates this in a clear, simple way, as his use of the word 'fable' in the essay indicates. It is a concept which runs through all his work, but in each novel he treats it in a totally different way and with increasing complexity.

He sums up his post-war adult life in two sentences in 'On the Crest of the Wave':

> I have never taught at a university and I know nothing about publishing; but I have taught English for twenty years in a large grammar school, and I have been trying to write the sort of thing I would define as 'Significant Literature' for longer than that. For fifteen years I travelled the countryside, lecturing in villages and hamlets, taking classes of adults in towns and cities and army camps. (*The Hot Gates* 126)

In addition to this, he reveals quite a lot about himself in his accounts of his travels on holidays and on lecture tours ('The Hot Gates' [*The Hot Gates*]; 'Egypt from my Outside' [*A Moving Target*]; 'Through the Dutch Waterways' [*A Moving Target*], etc.) His most recent book is *An Egyptian Journal* (1985). These travel writings give us many glimpses of his idiosyncrasies and his ways of responding to places and to people. In all these essays, and in the ones about ideas and books (whether his own or other people's), what is most interesting is his exploration of the development of his imagination.

1.2 BIOGRAPHY

William Golding was born in 1911. His childhood was spent in Marlborough where his father was a teacher at the Grammar School (this must not be confused with Marlborough School, which is a Public School, private, expensive, and far more prestigious than the local Grammar School). According to Golding the existence in the town of a Public School heightened the divisiveness of the class structure, which he says enrages him (interview with W. L. Webb, *The Guardian*, 11 October 1983). He once wrote that putting your son down for Eton is 'equivalent to stamping a coronet on the baby's bottom'. Nevertheless, he managed to write amusingly about the social stratification of a town very like Marlborough in *The Pyramid* (1967). The hierarchical social structure in *The Spire* has some historical justification, but the vividness with which it is presented probably owes something to Golding's experience of a correspondingly rigid structure in the twentieth century.

Though as a child he was a voracious reader of both English and Greek literature and was musically gifted, he went up to Oxford to read science. After two years he changed to English.

His first publication was a volume of poems (1934), now out of print. He spent some years as an actor and producer in a small company (providing a source for parts of *Pincher Martin*). He also did some work in adult education and in 1939, after his marriage, he took a teaching post at Bishop Wordsworth's School, Salisbury. After the outbreak of the Second World War, he left to join the navy, returning to the same post when it ended. At this time, he started writing steadily, but was repeatedly rejected by publishers: *Lord of the Flies* is famous in publishing history for having been rejected by more than twenty publishers before becoming a best-seller. He continued to teach, writing much of his next book, *The Inheritors*, in the school staff-room during free periods. He left Bishop Wordsworth's School in 1961 and spent the following year as writer-in-residence at a women's college in America. Since then he has devoted himself to writing and has confined his teaching to lecture tours and visits. He was awarded the CBE in 1966, he won the Booker Prize for *Rites of Passage* in 1980 and received the Nobel Prize for Literature in 1983.

1.3 GOLDING'S FICTION

Golding identified the starting point for his imaginative writing in 'Fable' (*The Hot Gates*, 87–9). The driving force behind his writing is his sense of the urgent need for human-beings to understand themselves and to cease to lay the blame for evil in the world on some outside power which they are unable to control.

Lord of the Flies (1954)

In this gripping novel, these problems are presented with the utmost clarity and simplicity. The boys invent a 'beast' to embody their fears and hatreds. Only Simon, the saint or 'Christ-figure', as Golding calls him in 'Fable', realises that the beast is 'us'. The other boys represent other facets of the argument, Piggy showing the inadequacy of the intellect to cope with the brutal aspects of human nature, Ralph the helplessness of the ordinary person (or even a somewhat exceptional one) when confronted by violence, and Jack and Roger exemplifying the human capacity for evil. This sounds very abstract and rather boring. It is not. Golding's great strength as a novelist lies in the way such abstractions are embodied in the vividly imagined world of the novel. *Lord of the Flies* combines the traditional virtues of a good adventure story – plenty of happenings, suspense, characters that seem recognisable and about whom we feel concern, and a setting which we can see vividly in our mind's eye - with a profound and disturbing challenge to our way of seeing human beings, including, perhaps, ourselves.

The Inheritors (1955)

This novel is an amazing imaginative experience in which the reader discovers what it might conceivably have been like to be Neanderthal man, woman or child. Instead of savages, Golding presents us with innocents. They can't think; they don't know good and evil; they don't hate or kill; they don't feel lust; they are not that 'diseased creation', man. Golding also shows us the 'new People', our forebears; they can think, they fear and kill and lust. In the final chapter we see through their eyes, read their language - and know we are back in our own world. Just as the boys in *Lord of the Flies* invented a 'beast' in order to externalise the beastliness in themselves, so the New People create a beast; they call the innocent, gentle Old People 'the red devils'.

In this novel, Golding has again separated goodness from evil, this time embodying the two qualities in the two groups of characters. Such simplification might seem damaging, but reading *The Inheritors* is such a wholly new imaginative experience that the simplicity - even triteness, as Golding suggests in 'Fable' - of the concepts seems irrelevant, even, perhaps, necessary.

Pincher Martin (1956)

This is another example of Golding's capacity to present his familiar ideas in a way which is utterly different from what he has done before. Again, the world he imagines is a strange one; a man is apparently, alone on a rock in the ocean. This time, the character is 'more fallen than most', according to Golding; he said (in an 'Introduction' to an American edition) that he had intended to make this fact absolutely clear and that he was appalled to discover that people found 'something heroic' in Pincher's struggles with the elements. This is probably the last novel he wrote with such an explicit didactic intention. After *Pincher Martin* he stopped insisting that only one interpretation - his own - was possible.

Free Fall (1959)

Free Fall marks that particular turning-point and some others. Throughout the novel, the central character is asking questions. Some are answered by implication, some not at all. This clearly signals a change from the single interpretation which had been the intention - but not wholly the effect - of the previous novels. It differs from them, too, in being set mainly in the everyday world of twentieth-century England. There is a variety of settings instead of the single, sharply focused locality of the earlier books.

This, combined with the unanswered questions, makes the novel more diffuse. It gains in complexity and ambiguity, but it loses that powerful concentration which makes such an impact on the imagination in the first three books.

The Spire (1964) and its successors

The purpose of these comments on Golding's other novels in a book about *The Spire* is to show that it is the culmination of his earlier work and to identify the qualities that are characteristic of his writing. While still dealing with questions of good and evil, this novel suggests the complexity and mysteriousness of such concepts. yet at the same time its form is even more concentrated and powerful than that of *Pincher Martin*. In *The Spire* he has combined the strengths of the previous novels and gone beyond them.

Of all his novels written since *The Spire*, *Darkness Visible* (1979) seems to me the most interesting, strange and disturbing. Goodness and evil are embodied in separate characters as in his early novels, but here they are mysterious and inexplicable. It is a complex, difficult novel; it intensifies our apprehension of Golding's world without clarifying it. It leaves the darkness 'all around, inexplicable, unexorcised, haunted' ('The Ladder and the Tree'). *Rites of Passage* (1980) is in form more akin to his early novels. Its setting (an early nineteenth-century sailing-ship) is again a restricted one. He makes particularly interesting use of the shift from one narrator to another, which in most of the novels comes at or towards the end.

Endings

Some knowledge of Golding's other endings helps to illuminate the end of *The Spire*. In the first three novels the switch from one point of view to another comes right at the end. Suddenly, we find we are looking not at a hunted human being but through the eyes of a naval officer at a little boy in a bedraggled school uniform (*Lord of the Flies*); not at a gentle, loving being whose sensations we share, but through the eyes of an intelligent but frightened person like ourselves at a small, hairy animal (*The Inheritors*). In *Pincher Martin* this shift begins to seem rather a gimmick. Two new characters are introduced in the final chapter to discuss and explain the central issues of the book. Are there such shifting perspectives in *The Spire*? Do they occur at the end? Are there occasions in other parts of the book where we suddenly ind that we are not looking with Jocelin but *at* him? A good ending often forces us to rethink our responses to the whole book. Does *The Spire* do this?

Golding continues to be able to surprise us. His latest novel, *The Paper Men* (1984) ends in the middle of a word.

2 *THE SPIRE* :
SUMMARIES AND CRITICAL
COMMENTARY

2.1 SYNOPSIS

The Spire is set in the thirteenth or fourteenth century in a cathedral town. The central action is the adding of a spire to the cathedral. Jocelin, the Dean, forces through the building work in spite of opposition from the other monks, from the builder, Roger Mason and from the verger, Pangall. The novel explores the implications and consequences of his determination to have his way. The process is presented as it is perceived by Jocelin; his consciousness is the central concern of the book.

2.2 INTRODUCTION

It is absolutely essential to read the novel at least twice before looking at this (or anybody else's) account of it. This is necessary with any work of literature, but the point has to be made especially emphatically with Golding's novels. Bewilderment is part of the imaginative experience he offers us. We need to feel our way towards an understanding before moving on to analysis and criticism.

The summary section of each chapter is intended merely as a quick reminder of the external events which seem to occur. The term 'external' is not wholly satisfactory since what we seem to be observing is almost entirely what Jocelin sees, and he is not a reliable observer or narrator.

2.3 CHAPTER SUMMARIES AND COMMENTARY

CHAPTER 1

Summary
The book starts with an introduction to all the main elements in the novel: Jocelin, the beginning of work on the spire and its effect on the surroundings, and many of the characters (Pangall (the verger), and Goody (his wife); Anselm and Father Adam (monks at the cathedral); the dumb sculptor, Jocelin's aunt and his ambiguous 'angel').

Commentary
This opening chapter requires very close study because it teaches us how to read *The Spire*. All the main themes are started here, and the main motifs which will echo through the book. At the same time we become aware that there is no clear view of any of these things. The first paragraph alerts us to the complexity of the way the story is told.

Like God in the stained-glass window, the book explodes at the reader in the opening sentences. The unnamed 'he' is caught in mid-action, so that in the first sentence we have a visual picture of a laughing man; in the second sentence, our view shifts and we see what he sees, the sunlight exploding through the glass, lighting up the images of Abraham, Isaac and God. Our sense of seeing through his eyes is intensified by the 'additional spokes and wheels and rainbows' formed by his tears of laughter. Golding is signalling, even in this first paragraph, that the vision is distorted.

He finds numerous ways of making the reader feel physically at one with Jocelin. His great height is suggested, not by making us look up at him but by making us look down with him at Pangall's 'dusty thatch' and Father Adam's tonsure. You will notice other ways in which we are made to recognise not only how tall he is, but how tall he feels. (It is worth considering, too, what is the effect of making this character a tall man, conscious of his height.) Similarly, as Jocelin 'looks round his nose', we begin to get the sensation of having a big nose ourselves, just as the effect on the knees of long spells of kneeling is felt, rather than noticed by an observer. Jocelin even 'felt a smile bend the seams of his own face' – a smile felt, not a smile seen. When Father Adam's toes get trodden on, it is with the treader not the trodden that we share the experience: 'he felt soft toes under his shod heel'.

Though Golding works to make us place ourselves imaginatively inside Jocelin's body, he also devises various means by which we are enabled to look at him from the outside and to catch glimpses of views and opinions other than his. This is an essential element in the novel and it has several effects. Golding stimulates our visual imagination through the device of the stone head. By making Jocelin scrutinise, comment on and question the accuracy of the carving, he is able to give a clear but changing picture, the dumb man's view and Jocelin's own being superimposed on one another, something like a Picasso head, where one view of a person seems imposed on another. The whole of this chapter (perhaps the whole of the book?) has a similar effect. We receive a clear impression which seems to change as we look at it as another impression is superimposed on it.

Dialogue, of course, is a way of bringing in a variety of points-of-views and attitudes. It is partly by this means that Jocelin's excitement about the beginning of work on the building is qualified and criticised. The first conversation , with the Lord Chancellor, immediately brings the whole scheme into question, with references to the immense height of the projected spire and the weakness of the foundation. Jocelin's weaknesses, too, are observed and commented on by the two deacons. His confident assumption that they are talking about somebody else reveals the very sin they were criticising – pride. His spurning of Father Adam's repeated attempts to catch his attention is indicative of his self-absorption. Even Pangall's talk of a man killed and of his own fears of being killed elicits only brusque responses. The aunt's letter makes the same point: ' "Can you not spare a word for me?" .' The only person he communicates with without reluctance is the one who can't reply, the dumb sculptor.

In these ways, the opening chapter swiftly creates an external view of Jocelin's appearance, of his behaviour and of his personality, even though almost everything we are told is what Jocelin sees, hears, says or thinks. Because of this, the occasional description of him as seen by the unspecified narrator carries great weight. The repeated references to 'laughing, chin up' begin to sound a little crazy, even if it is 'holy mirth'. More subtly, the hints of his self-delusion are given through the use of biblical quotations. They seem to suggest devoutness, but what are their implications? As he enters the side door into the cathedral, he always says to himself ' "Lift up your heads, O ye gates!" ' He is bowing his head at the time (remember his height) and we might well take this as an example of his piety – unless we know how Psalm 24 goes on – 'and the King of Glory shall come in'. Since he sees himself in the carving as an angel, the question of whose glory he is working for arises from the beginning of the novel. (There are several other occasions where he seems to be identifying himself with God or Christ.) His postponement of his prayers in order to see 'my daughter in God' raises suspicions of other motives, which increase when she turns out to be the one topic which he pursues with interest when talking to Pangall. His lack of concern with the services of the cathedral is suggested when he hears the music from the Lady Chapel as 'wah, wah, wah'. In these ways, even in the first chapter, Jocelin reveals motives concealed even from himself. Yet the ambiguity remains. The shifting nature of the readers' responses to him is reflected in the shifting pronouns, from 'he' to 'I' and back again. This creates a sense of uncertainty: we cannot be sure where we stand or whether the information we are receiving is reliable. We seem at one moment to be looking over Jocelin's shoulder, then just behind his eyes, then in his brain; even when the view of him appears to be external, there is often the suspicion that it is Jocelin's reading of that view which we are given.

The visible world is vividly presented, but here, too, there is no certainty about what is 'real': 'The most solid thing was light'. The dust and sunlight become honey, which becomes a pillar. The sun striking horizontally through the south windows is so powerful that Jocelin almost imagines that it comes from overhead and 'my stone ship lay aground on her side'. He is aware that this is an illusion and is amused to think how the mind 'deceives itself as easily as a child'. He is unaware, of course, of the tremendous significance of this thought, and so are we until the second reading. Nor does he attach any particular importance to his next thought – that the cathedral looks like a pagan temple where the workmen are 'priests in some outlandish rite'. The changes caused by the work are disorienting not only to the chancellor on his way to mattins, but to Jocelin and to the reader. The relationship of inside to outside is changed, so that what was far apart is now adjoining, the smooth inner walls adjacent to the rough outer walls. Pangall's cottage and yard are transformed by stacks of materials so that he complains ' "I can scarcely find my own door." '

In this shifting, changing world that Golding has created, readers have to be alert for every clue which may help to give them their bearings. The process is similar to reading a detective story; but our suspense and uncertainty as we attempt to follow the threads are more interesting and exciting because we are pursuing clues to questions of psychology and philosophy and expanding our imaginations, not merely discovering whodunnit (though it is a detective story too – it could have been called *The Mystery of the Missing Verger*, or even *Murder in the Cathedral* if T. S. Eliot had not got there first.) This first chapter trains us in ways of reading the whole book. I have given instances of a variety of ways of seeing which the text invites. You will find many others as you reread.

This densely packed opening chapter is necessarily expository, establishing the situation and introducing the main themes and characters. The basic facts are given, but in such a way that we have to pick them up through snippets of conversations and fragments of thoughts. We are plunged immediately into the life of the cathedral so that we learn obliquely of the existence of the model with its detachable spire, the projected height, the weakness of the foundations; there is no sense that we are being fed preliminary information. The statement that this is the first day of work on the new spire, 'a final beginning', is postponed until we have had a glimpse of the chaos and dissension it is causing, so that we are made aware of the struggle there has been to get to the starting-point. The attraction Goody holds for Jocelin, the taunting of Pangall by the workmen and his terror of them are quite explicit, but it is probably only at second reading that the hints about Pangall's impotence can be understood with any certainty. The significance of the aunt's money and how she acquired it is suggested in her letter, but no explanation is offered. Things which in many novels would seem to be mere matter of fact are here presented through hints and suggestions. We see what Jocelin sees, hear what he hears, but we become aware that there are things he doesn't want to see, hear or understand. Golding thus puts the reader in the position of continually conjecturing about these things and about Jocelin's reasons for suppressing them.

The motifs which recur throughout the novel appear in the first chapter simply as mysterious phenomena. Jocelin sees the model as a man lying on his back in the marsh, with the new spire 'springing, projecting, bursting, erupting from the heart of the building'; a little later, the building itself becomes a drugged body and he is a surgeon operating on it. He is not yet identifying himself with it, yet the two images, one of erupting vitality (the image is not explicitly phallic yet) and the other of unconsciousness and vulnerability, linger in the memory, to be awakened next time building and body become interchangeable. The angel at his back is both powerful and gentle, creates terror and joy, is a 'personality' yet 'it might have been in his very spine'. We can interpret it as an angel, a devil or tuberculosis of the spine.

Perhaps the most enigmatic of the recurrent motifs is the splash of Pangall's tear on Jocelin's instep, 'a wet star . . . that slid off the dubbin into the mud of the yard'. Jocelin reacts impatiently, looking away and up to where the spire will be. Later it will be mistletoe on his shoe which he will refuse to think about. The comparison of Pangall's cottage to the remnants of a swallow's nest 'hung in the angle of the yard against the cathedral wall' works in a similar way, like 'leitmotiv' in music. When we come to the later 'swallow's nest' inside the tower, this one may echo in our minds. On second reading, this first reference to the swallow's nest will certainly set up reverberations, anticipating the later references. In this way, the writer, like the composer, creates a sense of pattern, binding the whole work together. In these two instances, the links are made closer still by their connection with the pagan elements in the novel. The use of mistletoe in pagan religion and its role in the myth of Balder and the use of a jumble of materials to build the cottage (from 'ancient beam, wattle and daub' and Roman bricks to materials taken from the cathedral itself) establish the Christian verger's own connections with the pagan past now erupting into the present and making him its victim. At first reading we are, of course, unaware of these resonances.

I have highlighted the things we don't know and can't understand as we first read Chapter 1 of *The Spire*. I have even suggested that a sense of bewilderment is a necessary part of the experience of reading the novel. Yet from the first striking picture of the laughing man in an explosion of sunlight, there follows a series of extraordinarily vivid glimpses of different parts of the cathedral and the people in it, seen from all sorts of different angles. These impressions are not only visual. Noise reverberates through the chapter – the 'bat-thin' voice of the chancellor, the banging and shouting of the workmen, 'chink, snip' of the glass-cutters, the chanting of mattins. All these sounds 'would have been formless as the noises of the market-place' had they not been contained and shaped by the vaulted roof of the cathedral. Similarly the echoes started in this chapter will be picked up and given shape by the way they reverberate through the book.

A number of questions are raised by this first chapter. It is a demanding way into a book, but an exciting one, too. The absence of a fixed or reliable position from which to contemplate what the author has created is challenging and disorienting. This enables us to have an experience similar to that confronting the characters, disoriented by their changing surroundings.

Are there objections to this method? Is there any danger of the book seeming more like an itellectual puzzle than an imaginative experience? Are there disadvantages as well as advantages in making the reader work so hard? It would be unhelpful to ask oneself such questions at first reading, but after a second complete reading, it is a good idea to examine the ways you have responded to these methods, and to consider how far they have seemed an invitation to explore further or whether mere obscurity has been discouraging.

Chapter 2

Summary

The controversy about the building of the spire is crystallised in the quarrel between Jocelin and Anselm, which leads Jocelin to consider the human cost of his plan, yet he thinks, 'Cost what you like'. The pit gives Roger Mason final proof of the lack of foundations, but Jocelin insists that they 'dare' to build high. The promise of the Holy Nail seems confirmation of his vision.

Commentary

There is greater emphasis in this chapter on the external, on what can be observed. Jocelin's violent response to the hodman's song is in terms of gesture, not of thought. His rage is expressed in action. The striking verbs – 'hurried', 'peered', 'went poking and peering', 'clashed', 'wrenched' – are almost like stage-directions, creating a scene. The young man leaping, startled, to his feet, catching his falling book, acts out the reader's surprised response to Jocelin's violent behaviour. What follows is mainly in dialogue, thus firmly establishing readers in the position of an audience. Mood is conveyed by observable gestures – controlling the voice, clenching and unclenching the fist. The chapter consists mainly of a series of scenes between Jocelin and Anselm, Jocelin and Roger, with a monologue by Rachel. This would seem to make an unbiased view of the characters and situation possible. But though the speech seems genuine, the descriptions are coloured by Jocelin's attitude: 'Anselm coughed delicately, tuh, tuh, tuh' is not a bare statement of fact; 'delicately' and the repeated 'tuh' hint both at his veiled resentment and at Jocelin's suppressed contempt for his unarticulated complaints. Jocelin's ear may be very acute, or he may be imagining 'a hint of quotation round the wheel and the shoulder'. Golding uses this short passage of dialogue to highlight the contrast between the two men. Anselm's calm, controlled manner hides a tension which sometimes makes him tremble. His submissiveness in rising when Jocelin demands it and his obedient 'merest inclination of the head' seem to be calculated rebukes; he knows what he is doing and implying. Jocelin has no such knowledge and no self-control: 'some odd combination of causes was bringing Jocelin's blood to a rage'. This sentence illustrates the uncertainty about the position of the narrator which keeps recurring. It is expressed in the third person. Is it Jocelin who doesn't know the causes of his rage? Is the narrator signalling that the causes are unknown, perhaps unknowable?

Such ambiguities remain, even though this chapter does clarify some of the bewilderment created in Chapter 1. We begin to get a sense of a world existing independently of Jocelin's consciousness, of people having their own lives, opinions, wishes, frequently in opposition to his. After the tentative criticisms made in the first chapter, the whole cathedral now seems to be swarming with opposition. It is not in Jocelin's head, but out there, vocal, active, challenging. By using a lot of dialogue, by individualising the characters through their speech rhythms and vocabulary (compare the ways Anselm, Roger and Rachel speak), Golding builds up a sense of a busy, populated world. These are not complex psychological studies, but characters presented from the outside. The use of description and dialogue gives us a sense of observing them ourselves; we stand apart from Jocelin, who regards them as regrettably uninspired 'instruments' he must use. Their interests, their work, their relationships with one another, the things they talk about, the hints about the position of women in this world all help to create a sense of place and time that is quite specific.

It is not an historical novel in the conventional sense, but Golding does enable us to have a vivid idea of what it might have been like to live in a medieval town when a cathedral was being built. (Historians may argue that the way the cathedral was built was quite different from this; nevertheless, it is convincingly *imagined*.)

This raises the question of time in this novel. Is it concerned with a particular time in history? Is it timeless? Is it topical - for us, now? There will be some discussion on this in Chapter 3, but you should at this stage be considering your own impressions. Examine the discussion with Roger; the conflict between what is practical and what can be imagined bears directly on our own wonder at the achievements of cathedral-builders with their limited means. Jocelin's determination to have his 'invisible geometric lines' realised in stone, 400 feet up in the sky is the desire for the fulfilment of a particular vision at a particular time. But human beings have always tried to push beyond what seems possible. Jocelin's insistence on going higher than anybody has gone before certainly has parallels in our own day. Such challenges to what is accepted by most people always cause disturbance, there is always a price to pay. In Chapter 1 we were alerted to the tremendous cost in money. In this chapter, Jocelin begins to see that there will be other kinds of cost: ' "I thought you would cost no more than money but still cost what you like" '. Jocelin's single-mindedness is highlighted by his conversations in this chapter. The conflicts between his need for love and approval and his ruthless determination to have his own way is shown in the dialogue with Anselm. There is even a moment when, in spite of all, Anselm seems to be offering friendship; Jocelin rejects his offer, using his superior position to crush him, putting the spire above friendship, or even regarding it as a friend, since he talks to it (as yet unbuilt) addressing it as 'you'. Then the letter promising the Holy Nail arrives. In his excitement, with a characteristic mood-swing, Jocelin wants to be friends with Anselm again. When he is rebuffed, he thinks 'I must erase him'. Such bitter contempt for another human being was also suggested when he named Father Adam 'Father Anonymous'. People are nothing to him. His violent changes of mood, from love to contempt, from excitement to despair confirm our sense of Jocelin's mental instability, already hinted at by the laughter of the opening sentence, and perhaps now beginning to acquire a manic quality. He feels human beings are uncontrollable, so 'let them fall and vanish'. In his characteristic posture, chin up, he turns away from fallen humanity and seeks comfort in his angel and his vision in the sky.

In this chapter, Golding has focused mainly on the problems which Jocelin faces in the external world. At the same time he has suggested some of the aspects of his character which give him the driving-force to challenge all opposition. The fierceness and violence of his reactions to everything –

the hodman's song, Rachel's stream of talk, Anselm's rebuff, the Holy Nail, Roger's doubts - can be seen as the responses of an unbalanced personality out of touch with reality; at the same time, Golding raises the possibility that a refusal to accept a conventional view of 'reality' can lead to a widening of horizons, a discovery that what seems impossible can be achieved. The medieval cathedrals still stand. Madman or visionary? Or both?

Chapter 3

Summary
The time-span of this chapter is autumn to March. It is a winter of incessant rain which floods the vaults bringing the stench from the dead buried there into the cathedral. Jocelin learns why Rachel is childless, sees that a relationship between Goody and Roger has developed, and acknowledges for the first time that he knew Pangall was impotent. He is disgusted by Roger and Goody but also thinks 'She will keep him here'.

Commentary
It is interesting to notice how varied Golding's methods are. Before reading any further, glance through Chapters 2 and 3 and see in how many ways they contrast with one another.

Did you notice that Chapter 2 is largely in dialogue, while in Chapter 3 there is hardly any? In Chapter 2, people seem to Jocelin to be his main problem; in chapter 3 it is natural forces, especially the weather, and also his own feelings. In Chapter 2, sexual relationships were implied, treated obliquely through hints in the dialogue. Now they are presented explicitly, through outspoken dialogue and description.

The exploration of Jocelin's sexual feelings is similarly more explicit than before. Golding uses imagery to create a sense of his disgust, but first he gives a vivid description of the effects of the rain on the building and the town, emphasising the stench from the pit of the bodies buried beneath the cathedral and rotting in the swampy ground. The filth and the 'whiff of the pit' are emphasised throughout the chapter, so that we are conscious of their actual existence all the time. The metaphorical implications begin to be registered when Jocelin remembers, 'Here, where the pit stinks, I received what I received, all those years ago'. The idea that his vision may have some association with murky depths begins to be made explicit. But even while clarifying the point, Golding never presents it in terms of an abstract idea. The spire, made of solid stone and wood will stand directly above the pit, and its foundations must be down in the depth where the stench comes from.

In examining Jocelin's responses to the sexual attraction of Goody and Roger, Golding makes the fusion of the actual and the metaphorical even clearer. First he has presented the pit as a hole dug for a specific practical purpose, then it becomes a source of horror and fear not only because it exposes death and decay but also because it reveals the danger of implementing Jocelin's vision. Now it becomes a metaphorical pit 'inside Jocelin'. This pit is the source of his feeling that 'the renewing life of the world was a filthy thing, a rising tide of muck'. Here Golding makes us experience the metaphorical filth and muck so vividly because he has already made us feel we can see and smell the actual filth and stench. This is not to say that we even momentarily share Jocelin's view of the sexual relationship; rather, we have a sense of a mind filled with filth. He is not really looking at other people, but at himself. Golding gives a number of hints to show that this realisation is dawning on Jocelin too. He glimpses the implications of the way he is holding 'his folly' in his hands. The imagined blow in the groin and his cry of 'Filth' show that his disgust is more with himself than with its ostensible object, Rachel (after she has been so outspoken about her sex life).

In these ways the symbolism of the pit and the spire accumulates layer upon layer of meaning and feeling. In the first chapter, the cathedral corresponded in a fairly simple way to the body of a man. Now, fears about sex and death, about the unknown and the inexplicable have been added to the original image. Jocelin does not want to face these complexities, nor others, still suppressed, and so he talks to Pangall of the sons he will have and the glory of the cathedral they will be tending; he is even holding the model spire as he does so. Pangall naturally thinks that Jocelin, too, like the workmen, is taunting him because of his impotence.

This response at last forces Jocelin to recognise that Goody is married to an impotent man, though the full implications of this are withheld from the reader because Jocelin does not let them come into his consciousness yet. He realises that since both her marriage and Roger's are unsatisfactory, the sexual bond will keep Roger from departing with his workmen. Thus Jocelin sees the four of them as corresponding to the four pillars at the crossways, joining together to sustain his vision.

In the final paragraph, Golding uses the dream as a way of giving a clearer suggestion of Jocelin's subconscious motivation. The body which was like the church in Chapter 1 is now Jocelin's own: Satan 'clad in nothing but blazing hair . . . worked at the building'. His suppressed sexual feelings for Goody are thus made vividly clear without any direct statement or any admission of them into Jocelin's waking consciousness.

The intricate pattern of cathedral and model, characters and inner life forms a tightly-knit structure, in which the figurative and the actual are woven together. As the novel proceeds, we get a sense of tremendous weight being put on the symbolism of the cathedral. All the characters are 'built in' hardly anything is extraneous to the central image. The problems of structuring the book begin to seem to have something in common with the problems of building the spire.

Chapter 4

Summary
With the coming spring, the work continues busily; wood arrives from Ivo's father's land and simultaneously the near-illiterate Ivo takes time off from hunting to be made a canon. The workmen become restive, wanting danger-money. The movement of the earth in the pit demonstrates how great the danger is. Roger's desperate appeal to Jocelin to be released from the contract, and thus also from the adulterous tie to Goody is disregarded. In the midst of chaos and violence, the pit is filled in (with carved heads of Jocelin among the stones) and Pangall disappears. The dumb man saves Jocelin from being trampled to death.

Commentary
The pattern of contrast between the end of one chapter and the beginning of the next is continued here with an abrupt transition from the depths of Jocelin's subconscious mind to the external world, initially presented in an objective way. By the third sentence we are back in his consciousness, though the focus is still on the people and the places. We see what he sees; what he sees is affected by his changing states of mind and his angle of vision. The whole notion of objectivity is brought further into question since the wet weather has created the illusion that the cathedral is sinking into the earth. The 'sane factual thing, so many feet long . . . ' is just one other way of perceiving it.

Jocelin's continuing illusions about himself are suggested by his repeated use of Christ's statement, 'I am about my Father's business'. The repetition of this and of 'Lift up your heads O ye Gates!' (cf. Chapter 1) place a very sharp emphasis on Jocelin's delusions of grandeur. His gaze is fixed on the highest point of the building, turned away from all the human life around him. The images of framing (by the window and by the hole in the roof) are devices he uses to shut out everything that does not have direct bearing on his vision of the spire. Golding is perhaps also indirectly concerned with the novelist's similar problems of finding a way of shaping a novel. The question of how much of the multiplicity of the life of the town and how much of the individuality of the characters to let in is one which must be faced continually. Golding solves the problem by rigorous restriction or framing. This is exemplified in this chapter when Ivo is brought in to make a point. He is given no complexity since none is required to make that point, and is sent firmly back to his hunting. The parallel with Jocelin's position as dean and his lack of qualifications for it (see Chapter 11) is left clear and stark by the clear and concise treatment of Ivo. No explanatory comment is needed. He is a device, not a character, but the problem of plausibility is neatly solved by snatching him from the hunting-field to perform his function and returning him briskly to it as soon as he has fulfilled it.

The question of historical plausibility necessarily arises in this novel. Golding could have done a lot of research, finding out all that could be found out about medieval building techniques and then incorporated some of the detail in the novel. Instead of using this matter-of-fact and pedestrian approach, he solves the problem imaginatively. By seeing through Jocelin's eyes, as he watches uncomprehendingly while Roger plans and tests and measures, he is freed from the requirement of accurate reporting on the procedures. Critics who suggest that Golding got the historical facts wrong are dealing with irrelevancies, since it is Jocelin's anxious, impatient observation of the procedure on which we have to rely. We have found him an unreliable narrator in other spheres; there is no reason why he should not be equally unreliable on architecture.

In this way, Golding is able to avoid making claims for the factual accuracy of his account, while at the same time giving a vivid sense of what is going on in the cathedral. Roger's work with T-square and plumb-line, the noises, and the meetings of the workmen are ways of creating the impression of a world full of varied activities which exists quite apart from Jocelin's perception of it. Thus, quite sketchy and simple means are used to make us feel that we are watching a medieval cathedral being built.

We now come to the crucial episode of the pit, which will be discussed in detail (on p.64). It is noteworthy that during the previous night the connection between the angel and the devil at Jocelin's back has become especially close and his dreams have been 'particularly loathsome'. After the sight of 'the damned stirring' and the panic filling-in of the pit, the uncertainty about what is hellish and what is heavenly becomes more explicit. The heads of Jocelin which were to have been built in above the high windows of the tower are flung into the pit. He is 'built in' to the foundations literally and also figuratively since he now feels he is supporting the whole building on his back. The argument with Roger that follows is partly about the conflict over what can be seen to be feasible and rational and what is visionary; Jocelin sees it as a matter of having faith or not. But it is not possible to see Roger as the simple, rational man and Jocelin as the seer or visionary. Jocelin is determined to 'trap' Roger, to make him obey his ruthless will. He has several means of doing

this; he plays on the contract Roger has signed; he thinks of the connection with Goody and how he can use it to keep him at the cathedral;
and he uses the fear of unemployment for Roger and his men by claiming
that he has written to other cathedrals to forestall any attempt to get
work elsewhere. It is not clearly stated that he is lying; Jocelin is not
honest enough with himself to allow that into his consciousness. Instead,
his knowledge that he can save the spire in this way makes him 'tremble
from head to foot'. Nor does he let his guilt about using Roger's love for
Goody deter him, even when Roger begs to be forced to break the bond.
He admits into his consciousness the sight of Goody with her hair loose
and her white belly showing through the torn dress; he recognises Roger's
despairing acknowledgement that the bond between the two continues.
He admits hearing Pangall howling like a wolf as he runs from his pursuers
– and apparently that is all he knows about what happened to him. And it
is all we know as readers.

Our unreliable narrator, Dean of a cathedral, a man of faith and vision
has admitted to encouraging adultery, and using deception. It sounds like
a starkly honest confession. But Golding keeps the reader ignorant of what
it is that Jocelin knows and has repressed.

It is a good idea to examine your own responses to being treated in
this way by the author. Is it justifiable? What are the advantages of writing
a novel in this way? How does this gap in our knowledge affect the way we
read what follows? Reading any novel is a process of gradual discovery.
Golding (like many other novelists) withholds information in order that
the reader may experience the gradual unfolding. Consider this particular
instance especially in relation to Golding's use of Jocelin in the novel.

Chapter 5

Summary

In the aftermath of the creeping pit and singing pillars, Jocelin begins to
show overt signs of craziness. He deliberately detaches himself from people,
from his anxieties about Pangall and Goody and from the horror associated
with the mistletoe by climbing up the tower. From the top, where the new
heads carved by the dumb sculptor are soon to be added to the structure,
it is possible to see how the new building dominates and alters the landscape.
On his descent, Jocelin responds to the news of Goody's pregnancy with
a violent outburst of rage and weeping.

Commentary

Chapters 4 and 5 form a pair, Chapter 4 dealing centrally with the depths
of the pit and Chapter 5 with the top of the tower. In both, there are
carved heads of Jocelin. In between, at ground level (in the early parts of

Chapter five) is Jocelin with his living head which mysteriously takes on a life of its own: 'Jocelin's head preached . . . the sick head fell into . . . a sleep . . . when it woke up it knew . . . ' and, strangest of all, it was 'as if it had gone to ground for repairs rather than recovery'. The new strength, it is suggested, comes from underground. The use of 'it' instead of 'Jocelin' implies that he is not in control. His now 'blazing' certainty is combined with the 'high laugh' which is similarly uncontrollable. The laughter of the opening sentences of the novel has now become so definite a sign of mental disturbance that even Jocelin notices its oddity.

Increased madness and blazing certainty are associated with the hot autumn weather and the gargoyles gasping in the heat ('they were in hell'). Jocelin still feels himself as 'human, more or less' and feels human emotions, yet envisages himself as a partner in 'a necessary marriage' – to the spire. This, he hopes will enable him to avoid the complexities of human relationships and of his own psyche. Even so, his attempts to repress his puzzled obsession with Goody's red hair are unsuccessful and it constantly erupts into his consciousness. His gratitude to the young sculptor for saving his life becomes 'a sudden rush of love' as he hugs him; but as he does so, 'the red hair fell and blinded him'. This association of Goody and the dumb man recurs a number of times with several possible implications. Goody's horror of Jocelin ('not you *too*') marks her recognition of the sexuality of his feelings towards her. ' "What's all this?" ' he asks in response and climbs the spire (his marriage partner) to get away from the human 'cost of building materials' and the confusion within himself. In this way, Golding presents in physical terms the gap between himself and other people which Jocelin had created by refusing to notice them, looking upwards. He needs to escape also from the associations aroused by the mistletoe.

The rotting berry on his shoe 'set off a whole train of memories', but the only one mentioned is of the ship built of unseasoned wood. Golding does not make any reference to the use of mistletoe in pagan rites at Stonehenge, just over the downs, nor to the Norse myth of Balder who was killed with a mistletoe twig. The sense of horror and the use of the word 'obscenely' merely hint at these associations, but at second reading the berry on the shoe will act as a reminder of Pangall's tear on Jocelin's shoe in Chapter 1 and the sprouting, branching spire will point forward to later images of an alarmingly burgeoning plant-like spire. And the time will eventually come when Jocelin will admit the full implications of the mistletoe. Again, the first-time reader is in nearly the same position as Jocelin, puzzling over the implications of all this.

Nearly, but not quite the same position, because Jocelin's decision is to climb 'away from all this confusion'. This first ascent of the tower is a marked turning-point. The physical change that has come about is made visual by the new, leaner head carved by the sculptor, paralleling Jocelin's increasingly abnormal behaviour. When he ties up the skirts of his habit for climbing, one of the workmen 'knuckling his forehead' in the conventional sign for 'barmy' makes clear that Jocelin's increasing mental disturbance is reflected in his physical appearance. Up the tower, Roger 'examined him slowly from the toes of his shoes along the shins, the white thighs, up past the body to the face'. This minimal statement implies a lot. Seeing Jocelin through other eyes, we are enabled to visualise the change on which Roger comments, which corresponds to the inner veering towards madness.

Yet it is in this chapter that hints begin to suggest that we question that madness. The 'white impropriety of the thighs' becomes 'proper' at the top of the tower. The mad laugh expresses 'pleasure for the new things and the miracle'. Even in the midst of exulting in being free from the confusion down below, Jocelin develops a sensitivity towards Roger, understanding more of his problems now and recognising that he must be kinder to him. He even has a momentary memory of things repressed since the earth moved in the pit - Pangall being taunted and the 'fall of red hair' which accompanies all his memories. It is only a glimpse of Pangall but he admits 'it's the cost!', and even asks for mercy.

At the top of the tower, though, the contrary mood of exaltation is the dominant one. Golding stresses the sense of height, the feeling of being like a bird, of moving towards the clouds. He makes Jocelin long for even greater height so that he could 'oversee' (note the verb - not 'see over') 'the whole country'. He has a twinge of guilt over this, and a bigger one when he sees the downs as a young body: ' "I bring my essential wickedness even here into thy air" '. But his penitential prayer is a highly ambiguous one, not confessing to lustful imaginings but apologising for seeing beauty in the earth instead of horrors, and for valuing anything other than the cathedral.

His second look at the landscape is a second vision of power, for the tower has become a focal point, attracting travellers so that the winding tracks now steer straight for the city. Jocelin sees a new lesson 'for this level', the lesson that 'men blunt like a poor chisel'. This leads him to look down to Pangall's kingdom and the world of people far below, people sitting in the privy, watering the milk, lying drunk in the gutter or loitering in the inn instead of bringing the stone for the building. Jocelin fears the world below - ' "Here is my place" ' - but he cannot live with the eagles, and descent to earth brings him face to face with Goody's pregnancy and his own jealous rage and misery. His rage is ostensibly directed towards the carrier at The Three Tuns, and he pretends, even to God, to praise Him for Goody's fertility.

Throughout the chapter, and with especial concentration in the last few paragraphs, Golding uses the whole building from pit to spire as a metaphor for the extremes of human capability. Jocelin is 'built' in the same way, as a figure which embodies the extremes of human potential being both the visionary who can achieve new things and the mad or wicked man guilty of lust, hate, contempt and destructiveness. But the building is never reduced to a diagram of human contradictions. Though Jocelin continually sees it as a diagram, he also recognises that his 'few simple lines on the sky' have become solid wood and stone and that his tools are human flesh and blood.

Chapter 6

Summary
As the tower reaches its full height the singing of the pillars increases and Roger gives a graphic description of how it will split open if a spire is added. Jocelin's insistence forces Roger to come up with a technique for preventing this. Jocelin overhears Roger and Goody making love in the swallow's nest. In his horror he almost admits to himself his guilty involvement.

Commentary
Much of this chapter is concerned with building problems. Golding gives vivid detail of the actual processes, from minutiae such as the adze marks on the beams to a sight of the whole structure: 'Let your eye crawl down like an insect foot by foot'. In this way, the layers of meaning which we have been accumulating are now expressed almost wholly in terms of the actual and physical.

This is one of the sources of Golding's power as a novelist. His ability to make us imagine, to see, to hear, to have the sensation of being on the spot works so well because it is combined with the mysterious, the unstated, the inexplicable. The fact that we move to and fro between these two worlds makes each of them more vivid to our imagination. We also have to be alert to the echoes Golding sets up. The eye crawling down from the top of the tower to the bottom parallels Roger's scrutiny of Jocelin in the previous chapter from the toes of his shoes, up past his shins and thighs to his face.

The discussion about the next stages of the building is significant in other ways. On the one hand, Roger is explaining the problems he faces as a builder in practical terms. At the same time, Golding plays on the word 'mystery', setting its medieval meaning of 'craft' alongside hints of its modern meaning. Roger's description of precisely how the building is likely to split apart is a vivid imaginative exercise – so vivid that Jocelin actually sees, feels, hears it disintegrating under his feet.

Here Golding illustrates something he has hinted from time to time throughout the book. The parallel between constructing a spire and constructing a novel hovers behind much of the description of the planning and calculating that the work entails. Structuring, shaping, balancing one thing against another while continually daring to explore new regions, to soar imaginatively into the unknown, are aspects of the art of writing as well as of the art of architecture. Roger's description of the collapse of the spire is succinct and vivid. Jocelin, like an imaginative reader, recreates it in his imagination, sensuously experiencing it almost as if it were an actual event. But he also grasps the necessity of challenging this powerful story. He starts by classifying it as a ghost story told to frighten children. Then he tells his own story, of his vision, revealed to him, by God. By going to the highest authority of all, he is able to demolish Roger's version of the outcome of the enterprise. In his account, the building becomes a diagram of prayer, Roger is in a net, not Jocelin's, but God's net; the spire is admittedly a Folly, not Jocelin's, but God's Folly. The challenge of faith to what is reasonable is made with panache.

Jocelin is surprised at his own eloquence and at some of the enigmatic and threatening things he has said. He attributes them to 'the devouring Will, my master', which certainly qualifies his claims of divine inspiration. Roger thinks he is the devil himself, thus the two extremes, the heavenly and the hellish, are sharply juxtaposed, but not in a simple, diagrammatic way. The suggestions are tentative. Jocelin's growing anxiety about the building generates growing fears about his own motives. This response to the pressures arising from the arguments about the dangers of the building with Roger and about finances with the Chapter. seems appropriate to his individual psychology as it has been shown so far in the novel. His determination to manipulate Roger and control the building-works is contrasted with his inability to control his laugh or the 'images of the spire, of red hair, of a wolf howl' which sometimes 'float', sometimes 'storm' through his mind. While treating Jocelin's problems in this way, Golding also, by implication, raises more general questions about human aspirations and what drives people to great struggles and dangerous feats. Jocelin's attribution of responsibility to external forces, to God or to 'the devouring Will, my master' is something people in power are prone to in any period. Such people, whether in the religious or the political or any other sphere will excuse their ruthlessness in executing their plans by reference to some outside necessity such as divine justice, the state of the economy or the demands of the voters. This is a theme which runs through many of Golding's books. In *The Spire* the question of both good and evil arising from mixed human motives is explored.

Golding uses Jocelin's glimpse of the love-making in the swallow's nest to heighten our sense of his bewilderment and pain. He suggests Jocelin's chaos of feelings first by describing the physical effect on him, then the surge of memories of Goody (done with the utmost brevity as a list) and of his part in her marriage and her relationship with Roger. Finally, most effectively, he uses Rachel's 'gabbing and clacking' to suggest their mutual incoherence and dismay. For the first time, she actually impinges on Jocelin's consciousness, and he turns 'to bless her from his pain to hers'. At the end, he is like one of the stone heads, mouth open, eyes open, 'staring at nothing'.

It is worth examining closely the language and sentence structure of these last few paragraphs. Notice the rhythm of the sentences and their length, the use of direct speech and indirect speech. Consider how these serve to suggest the mental and emotional experiences Jocelin is undergoing.

Chapter 7

Summary
Jocelin feels linked to Goody, Roger and Rachel in 'some unholy marriage'. Roger's plan of binding the top of the tower in a steel band is achieved. Jocelin discovers to his horror that the tower is swaying and that this is the cause of the pillars singing. Jocelin arranges for Goody to be sent to a nunnery as a fallen woman. As he goes to take her the money for this purpose he encounters Rachel driving her husband from the cottage. Jocelin's appearance in the doorway precipitates a miscarriage and the death of Goody.

Commentary
In Chapter 6 the main focus was on the external world - the building process, the affair of Goody and Roger. Jocelin's feelings were often presented indirectly. This chapter is primarily concerned with exploring Jocelin's mental and emotional state. His obsession with her red hair and his failure to direct his thoughts elsewhere lead to an important development - his admission to himself of the mixture of 'dear love and prurience' in his attitude to her. The episode in the swallow's nest broke through the defences Jocelin continually builds up against knowledge of himself and of the world. Hearing and almost seeing Roger and Goody making love is too much even for Jocelin's powers of suppression. The 'watershed' mentioned at the beginning of Chapter 5 after the riot was the beginning of this process of self-discovery. What happens now confirms things we had already glimpsed and tentatively interpreted. The use of parallels keeps the reader looking backward and forward in the text. Sending Goody to a nunnery now corresponds to the earlier act of mar-

rying her to an impotent man. This method is effective in making Jocelin's psychological state convincing, since Golding has made us work at it ourselves, providing our own tentative interpretations as we read.

He also makes us see it both from the outside and from the inside. He mingles suggestions of Jocelin's behaviour – he is 'bent into a little grey space', he repeats words constantly, he talks to people who don't know what he is talking about, cries out but doesn't know what he has said – with accounts of what is happening in his head. The red and green of Goody's hair and clothes and 'storm', 'chaos' and 'whirlwind' are images to help us enter into his strange experiences, to have the sense of feeling what he feels. Then Golding does the opposite of this; he gives Jocelin a moment of lucidity in which he sees himself as perhaps the reader sees him. First, he realises that if he went to see Goody, he would 'ask and pry and demand without knowing what he wanted'; then he suddenly sees himself almost as if he were looking in a mirror. This also enables Golding to give a clear picture of his physical appearance – an advantage in the midst of so much mental turmoil.

The next stage of the building is treated in a new way. It is a skilled and dangerous operation, binding the top of the tower with a steel band to prevent it from bursting apart under the weight of the spire. By making Jocelin observe it from a distance, Golding is able to give a plausibly impressionistic account without having to go into minute technical detail. You might find it interesting to compare this method with the more detailed description elsewhere (for example, in Chapter 9). Which method is more effective in enabling you to see what is happening in your mind's eye?

The terrifying experience of realising the tower is swaying is a vividly visualised moment, with the sixth counter sliding into view hundreds of feet below. It is this ability to make us feel we are in a particular place and then to register precisely what we see that makes reading Golding's novels an imaginatively sensuous experience. After all, he could simply have told us, as he does later, that Jocelin 'knew that the tower was swaying under him like a tall tree'. That would have given us the sensation but not the experience of discovering it. (But note the words 'under him'; what difference would it make if they were omitted?)

The chapter ends violently with Goody's miscarriage and death. Jocelin's tentative growth in self-knowledge at the beginning of the chapter is given a violent shock. Buried things come to the surface confusedly; he recognises his sins, his cruelty, the 'dreadful glow' of his will. He seems to conclude that his motivation has been his love for Goody, yet he expresses it ambiguously in the words of a hymn. Golding conveys the mental agony and confusion. Is he offering a simple explanation of Jocelin's motives?

Chapter 8

Summary
Jocelin's physical and mental condition deteriorates, his back becoming more bowed, his behaviour more bizarre. Roger is now dominated by Rachel and drinking heavily; the pillars at the crossways start bending and he retreats in terror. The work goes on, with Jocelin being treated as a lucky mascot by the men who go to Stonehenge to celebrate midsummer with pagan rites.

Commentary
There is a change in method in the first part of this chapter. The previous free transitions from third to first person and back again are replaced by a clear typographic distinctions between them. The narrative is now presented wholly in the third person; thoughts are expressed in the first person, either enclosed in brackets (the repetitive, crazy ones) or in inverted commas as though they were spoken aloud, as they sometimes are, or in italics. There is a passage in the second person and one in the first person plural when Jocelin addresses his own image in the metal sheet.

Before reading further, it would be a good idea to consider what kinds of effects are created by sharpening the divisions between the different methods of presentation in this way.

One of the effects is to make us take our stance outside Jocelin, seeing him displaying the mannerisms of someone in the throes of a mental breakdown, repeating himself, adopting strange postures, disregarding attempts to communicate with him. This naturally has a slight distancing effect so that, for instance, the masturbatory fantasies (or torments of Satan) are reported by the narrator, not confessed by Jocelin. The distinction between the character we seem to watch and the one communing with himself (in brackets) serves as preparation for his sight of himself in the metal sheet when he talks to himself as 'Jocelin'. This scene, with its hints of schizoid illusions, is also a vivid example of the devices used by Golding to give a visual impression of Jocelin at each stage of his development. As with the stone heads, the attention to detail is natural because of Jocelin's surprise at the change in himself. Another effect of the juxtaposition of the narrator's description to Jocelin's madly repetitive thoughts is to give the reader the feeling of being rapidly switched from one mode of perceiving to another, almost with a jerk. This corresponds to the jerky, irrational, disconnected mode of Jocelin's thinking, so that Golding is able to set going in our heads similar thought processes. Consider, in this connection, the repeated italicised, *'What's this called? And this?'*, the second time interrupting a sentence – and a thought.

Yet, however often Jocelin cringes away from admitting certain things to himself, Golding is pushing him inexorably towards self-discovery. The fires on the horizon force him to recognise that the workers, 'his good men' are pagan, Devil-worshippers, and that the 'obscene' berry he saw on his shoe was mistletoe, used in the pagan rites and as a sacrificial tool. The knowledge of Pangall's death (and his own failure to intervene) is still repressed. He tries to escape responsibility by claiming, ' "I am bewitched" '.

In these ways, Golding on the one hand depicts a mind disintegrating as rational connections and coherence disappear from Jocelin's speech, thoughts and behaviour, and on the other hand, he makes some suggestion that this process is not entirely destructive, that through it Jocelin may actually be moving towards greater insight into himself and into the nature of the world around him. Though Golding takes a dismissive view of psychology, he, like many other imaginative writers, shares perceptions derived from twentieth-century psychological studies.

Chapter 9

Summary
Jehan has to organise the final dropping-into-place of the wooden framework without Roger, who has disappeared. The Visitor arrives and questions Jocelin about his vision and his behaviour. During a violent storm, Jocelin struggles up the spire and hammers in the Holy Nail.

Commentary
Chapter 9 might be described as a particularly medieval chapter. First there is the final stage of the building. The procedures are described in some detail, but I have not been able to find anyone who has a clear understanding of the technicalities. I have tried, unsuccessfully, to follow the account in my mind's eye and I have consulted an architect who was equally unsuccessful. Perhaps a boat-builder would be able to help since Golding says he merely glanced at a book on tower-building and then based his account on his knowledge of seamanship, which entails moving heavy things by primitive means. His use of the image of the cathedral as a stone ship with the spire as its mast confirms that such analogies were in his mind as he wrote. In other parts of the book, confusion has been due to Jocelin's uncertain vision. Here the intention seems to be to give a clear picture; if so, Golding has not succeeded. Nevertheless, I think he does create a sense of the medieval world and perhaps of the medieval mind in this chapter. The struggle to work on the swaying spire in the gale, the headlong flight of the workmen as the octagon crashes into position are described with brilliant clarity.

The arrival of the Visitor and the interrogation provide further occasion for emphasising aspects of the medieval church. The formalities of the visit are highlighted by Jocelin incongruously appearing with woodshavings in his hair (Anselm - spitefully? - having said, 'Why shouldn't he see him as he is?'). Such small details as the row of sandals under the table which Jocelin notices when he is supposed to be concentrating on the questioning give a particularly intimate sense of the period. The townspeople, too, make a brief appearance. This is one of the few occasions when we see them close at hand; usually they are looked down on, seen by Jocelin from high above. He is now in the midst of them, accused, held to be responsible for the apparently imminent fall of the spire. This sudden irruption emphasises how remote from ordinary life Jocelin has been, and gives a brief glimpse of the relationship of the ordinary people to the church dignitaries. Previously this has only been indicated through Jocelin's disapproval of Rachel's self-assertiveness and outspokenness, which he compares unfavourably with Goody's submissiveness and shyness. That implied comment on the position of women did not give a sense of that world as a whole. Here, too, the pleading voices, the grabbing hands, the thrust beard, are mere fragments.

What is the effect of keeping the life of the town remote from the main focus of attention in the novel? Are there advantages in this? Think about the structure of the novel as you consider this question. (Golding is said to have pared away a lot of material as he wrote.)

The discussion with the Visitor make explicit many of the issues raised by the novel. It encompasses a wide range, from the question of money to a consideration of the nature of vision. Up to this point, the novel has suggested an ambivalent, if not hostile, attitude to Jocelin's vision, emphasising the cost in human life and suffering and the suspect nature of his motives. The Visitor's unexpected sympathy shifts the balance towards a heroic view of the enterprise. In spite of his severe questioning about the pagan rites, the criminal workmen, the failure to go to confession, he maintains a sympathetic attitude. His insight into the unavoidable complexities arising from Jocelin's ambition indicates an awareness that high aspirations are likely to be mixed with egotism on a grand scale. He makes Jocelin understand 'to what a height a mind must climb' if it were to answer his questions about the nature of vision. It cannot be said that *The Spire answers* such questions but it does raise them in an exciting and imaginative way.

Contrasted with this rational discussion is Jocelin's inner life. Up to this point, his inner turmoil has been presented in terms acceptable to twentieth-century readers. Golding now switches to medieval terminology. He first uses the violence of the storm to create chaos and confusion of a natural kind. Jocelin is knocked about by the wind, the skirt of his gown lashes him, a lath strikes him on the thigh. It is only after he has been subjected to natural forces that Golding unleashes the supernatural in the form of beasts pawing at the windows. There are even howling creatures with scaly wings, but by making Jocelin wonder whether he is howling himself, he allows the twentieth-century reader to see them as purely interior experiences. The violence, even melodrama of these passages seem to me fully justified. They capture something of the grotesqueness of gargoyles or of the painting of Hieronymus Bosch (c.1450–1516).

Similarly, the Holy Nail brings together what is essentially medieval with modern ideas on psychology – or, arguably, with timeless psychological problems. It is, of course, one of those dubious relics ('part of the true cross') which played such an important part in church finances in the middle ages. Jocelin's trust in it is questioned by the Visitor's hinted incredulity and (in Chapter 10) by Alison's satirical laughter. It has other, suppressed, implications for Jocelin. When the song 'For want of a nail' eventually surfaces in his consciousness, he realises that his passionate concern about it is inextricably bound up with his feelings for Goody. This adds another psychological dimension to his later act (Chapter 10) of 'nailing the spire to the sky' (it was meant to go in its box at the base of the cross). The phallic symbolism is not quite explicit here, but his words to the spire. 'You might have fallen for want of it' suggest that he imagines himself in a state of permanent erection. He sees Goody as both devil and innocent, child and naked woman, female and male (being partly the dumb man 'humming from an empty mouth') while remaining a devil whose face he cannot see. At the same time this is 'uncountry' where there is 'consent and no sin'. This is a wonderfully concentrated passage, full of complexities and uncertainties. Jocelin's complicated sexuality is condensed into a single image suggesting not only heterosexual lust for the woman (forbidden to him as a priest) but also paedophilia (throughout, images of Goody as a child have been prominent) and homosexuality (or bisexuality) in his fusion of Goody and the dumb man (cf. Chapter 10: 'He knew how the shame included the dumb young man'); the devil is there too, so guilt remains. That it all takes place in 'uncountry' perhaps undercuts the sense of atonement; the longed-for union is taking place nowhere but in Jocelin's mind (but compare the reference back to this passage in the last pages of the novel.)

Chapter 10

Summary

This chapter deals with revelations – of Alison's part in Jocelin's advancement, of the hollowness of the pillars (seeing this, causes Jocelin's collapse) and of the crookedness of the finished spire.

Commentary

With the completion of the spire, there is a change of focus. Time now ceases to be treated chronologically. Jocelin is 'in the grip of new knowledge' but the centre of this chapter is Jocelin's vision, written many years before and itself referring back to the time by the sea when he was very young. The reading of it is intercut with his comments on it. This gives a condensed view of his development, so that there is a double time-scheme, one giving a bird's-eye view of Jocelin from his youth, the other being the almost day-to-day (or at least season-to-season) account of the past two years which we have been reading and are still engaged in reading. This suggests how much (and how little) he has changed. He is becoming more aware of other people, noticing minute details of Alison's appearances, even the water on her eyelashes, and the 'delicate calligraphy' of Father Adam's face. He even overcomes his pride and appeals for help, though this is immediately qualified by his inability to take Father Adam's criticism, demanding ' "And *my* prayer, Father? My – vision?" ' Most important of all is his recognition of the simplicity of his original vision and his growing awareness that life is far more complex and mixed than he had thought. The image of the riotously twining plant with faces entangled in it will continue to express his developing apprehension of the nature of things, a view far removed from his original, simple vision.

Chapter 11

Summary

Seeing the apple tree and the kingfisher is the key event of this chapter. It also deals with Jocelin's search for forgiveness (from Anselm and from Roger) and his confession that he knew of Pangall's impotence before the arranged marriage, and of his death. He admits his sense of guilt about Goody's death. Roger thinks Jocelin is trying to force a confession of involvement in the murder of Pangall.

Commentary

As the book moves towards its conclusion, the process of illumination speeds up, and Jocelin's sense of urgency grows as he approaches his death. His attempts to attain forgiveness are both failures, but between them comes the moment of the appletree and the kingfisher. The conversation with Anselm gives another quick recapitulation of salient events since the vision at the seaside, pin-pointing the parallel between Ivo and Jocelin, bringing into question not only his status as Dean but also giving another view of his vision, as an adolescent enthusiasm.

Jocelin repeats his cry for help, but the complexities suggested by the recurring plant images (cf. Chapter 10) cannot be resolved by Father

Adam. The sinister plant is replaced by the appletree with its blossom like
a cloud of angels, yet with 'a long black springing thing' among the leaves.
The recognition that 'there was more to the appletree than one branch' is
coupled with the flash of the kingfisher. Both tree and bird are perceived
with dazzling vividness by Jocelin. This realisation of the beauty of the
natural world makes him aware of how narrow-minded he has been, while
the black branch suggests that he is growing beyond what William Blake
called 'single vision'.

As he begins to see how complex and contradictory his own motives
have been, he switches from wondering whether 'all I was doing was
bringing ruin and breeding hate', to suggesting that Goody bewitched
him, to thinking, 'it may be the true Nail after all'. His image of himself
as 'a building with a vast cellarage where the rats live' and his plea for
Roger's forgiveness parallel and contrast with his previous plea to Anselm.
This emotional reconciliation is juxtaposed to Anselm's cold formality.
Both attempts are, of course, failures, one because of Anselm's refusal
of personal involvement, the other because of an excess of it, each partici-
pant being so wrapped up in his own guilt that he cannot grasp what the
other is trying to convey. Jocelin's clear reference to the murder of Pangall
seems to Roger an accusation and a demand for a confession. While Jocelin
urgently tries to find out if Goody colluded in the murder, Roger inter-
prets his confused words as a confession of love for her; Jocelin's claim
that 'I killed her as surely as if I'd cut her throat' brings Roger to a frenzy
of rage and jealousy. None of this is explicit and it is open to other interpretations. Jocelin's broken sentences and Roger's almost monosyllabic
interjections create the violence and bewilderment of the scene. We cannot
be sure what is going on, just as two people in a quarrel may be aware of
rage and passion without understanding the reasons for their mutual
antagonism.

Chapter 12

Summary
The book concludes with the precarious survival of the spire, Roger's
attempted suicide and consequent imbecility, and the dying of Jocelin.

Commentary
This final chapter does not work towards definition or even clarification.
It is partly a kaleidoscopic repatterning of all the elements of the novel,
but it is not merely retrospective; the sense of moving forward, of development continues until the final, 'It's like the appletree', with the last
paragraph containing a typical Golding shift in viewpoint, in this novel
done with the utmost brevity, simplicity and ambiguity. On the last page

he makes all the contradictions into a multiple vision of spire, tree, upward waterfall, girl, man.

So in this last chapter we are not looking for explanations. It is a process of further exploration, of holding multiple ways of seeing in our minds simultaneously, of recognising how the varied images all come together to create one composite, concentrated, enigmatic image.

Thus, the mystery remains, perhaps increases. For instance, until this chapter, the position in time had been clearly registered; the season, even in the month had been stated. But now, though there is a brief reference to sunlight and shadow measuring the hours, we have moved into a mode of time where seconds and centuries are indistinguishable. The references to centuries create the impression that Jocelin has moved outside time, 'until he knew that the great revolution of his clock was accomplished'. This image both suggests the ending of time for Jocelin and picks up the notion of his struggling heartbeat – that clock which will soon stop ticking for ever. The existence of the spire, too, is both timeless and time-bound. The reply to 'Has it fallen?' is always, 'Not yet'. Jocelin's sense of experiencing centuries is another link with the spire, centuries old now but some time bound to fall.

Similarly, after the precision of the town, the close, the cathedral, the spire, place becomes nebulous. The first answer to Jocelin's question (itself ambiguous) 'Where was I then?' is 'Nowhere'; the second time it gets no reply at all. This disorientation in time and space contributes to the uncertainties of this final chapter. Jocelin is still developing, but still erratically. He sees Father Adam's face now 'fully in focus' and he thinks, 'If I could go back, I would take God as lying between people and to be found there'. Yet he sees Father Adam and all people as naked creatures and thinks 'God knows where God may be'. The dumb man's new carving reduces Jocelin, too, to a mere stripped skeleton, mouth still open, recalling the eagle-like heads with mouths uttering hosannas.

Each attempt to reach some kind of conclusion is followed by a perception of its illusoriness. But it is not a movement entirely towards despair. The pictures of Roger imbecilic after his suicide attempt, Pangall buried in the pit and the spire damaged and crooked are followed by the more ambiguous vision of 'a tangle of hair blazing among the stars' and 'the club of the spire lifted towards it'. Even at the point of death, Jocelin sees his hope of heaven as meaningless 'unless I go in holding him by one hand and her by the other'. This reference to the 'uncountry' (see the end of Chapter 9) with its sense of atonement is qualified by 'I traded a stone hammer for four people'. But then this, too, is replaced by the final vision; the spire is 'still and silent but rushing upwards'; it is like a girl, a plant, a waterfall. In a mixture of exultation and terror, Jocelin becomes a bluebird, his life a moment of brilliance speeding into darkness. 'It's like the appletree' brings everything together – the beauty of the spire is like the beauty of nature, the appletree with its implications of good and evil is also the appletree of Chapter 11, with its angel blossoms and 'black springing thing'. Even in his account of his intentions in *The Spire*, Golding calls the spire 'the heart of some huge question' (*A Moving Target*, 166).

The last paragraph shifts the point of view (in a characteristic Golding ending) briefly making us see Jocelin's death from the outside. There is a strange quiet after all the shouting and excitement. The misinterpretation of the dying murmur, the exercise of charity, the giving of the Host form a fittingly ambiguous ending to the book.

3 WHAT *THE SPIRE* IS ABOUT: A CONVERSATION

With acknowledgements to Henry James's '*Daniel Deronda*: A conversation'. The characters are descendants of his Theodora, Pulcheria and Constantius.

*   *   *

One day in the autumn term, Connie was sitting in the refectory feeling deflated. She had stayed up half the night preparing her seminar paper on *The Spire* and now the tutor had 'flu and the group had dispersed. To her relief, she saw Helen and Theo, loaded with books and coffee, coming towards her corner. 'Hi!' said Helen, 'Cheer up! You've got a week's reprieve'. 'Worse luck!' replied Connie, 'I'd far rather get it over today. The feeling that I've horribly simplified the whole book is beginning to set in already. By next week . . . Any way, talking about what a thing means always seems to reduce it to a few simple ideas.'

3.1 COMPLEX OR SIMPLE?

HELEN: I should have thought that was your problem from the start. It *is* a few simple ideas – all Golding's usual things – 'the darkness in men's hearts' from *Lord of the Flies*, the cellarage from *Pincher Martin*, 'man is a morally diseased creation' – it's all summed up in 'Fable' (*The Hot Gates*, 85-101).

THEO: That really is reductive. Even when he was writing 'Fable', he said he didn't see things in the simple terms of *Lord of the Flies* any more. By *The Spire* he's creating really complex human beings. But I don't see why you're making a fuss about discussing the themes, Connie.

CONNIE: Once you start trying to say what a book's about, you're isolating one element and everything seems to come apart. ✓

HELEN: I'd agree if it were a really complex novel, but it's all so simple and diagrammatic. Jocelin was quite right when he called the spire a diagram – it is, and so is *The Spire*. The pit equals all the murky instincts down in the id and the spire is just phallic. It's simple, it's diagrammatic, it's hackneyed.

THEO: You're just saying this to provoke an argument.

3.2 GOOD AND EVIL

HELEN No. You must admit that Golding is obsessed by one idea – that man is diseased.

THEO: And why not? After Belsen and Hiroshima . . .

HELEN: But humanity is capable of creating other things besides
√ holocausts. It's not *only* 'darkness in men's hearts'. There's a kind of complacency in sitting back and saying 'Just admit we're evil and then . . . ' Then what? All our problems will be solved?

CONNIE: We certainly couldn't do anything about them without self-knowledge.

HELEN: It doesn't seem to do the world much good in Golding's novels. People are dead or barmy by the time Jocelin gets round to a bit of self-knowledge. Perhaps it enables him to die happy – does it? – but it doesn't do anything for the rest of them.

THEO: But you're asking for the kind of didactic, 'message' book that you'd be the first to complain about.

CONNIE: Anyway, most books worth reading have some idea embedded in them somewhere. It doesn't have to be a 'message'. I was trying to get a title for my seminar talk out of what Golding said about myth: 'Myth is something that comes out from the roots of things in the ancient sense of being the key to existence, the whole meaning of life and experience as a whole'.

HELEN: He's really pretentious in his essays, isn't he?

CONNIE: But they're very useful – when you feel confused, they're a lifeline. Then you can go back to having your imagination stretched in the novels, but with a bit more understanding.

THEO: So your argument is that *The Spire* provides 'the key to existence'?

CONNIE: I don't much like the sound of that . . .

HELEN: The trouble is that his novels seem to raise big questions about the nature of existence and to imply that an answer is possible.

THEO: That's certainly what he was aiming at. He answered a questionnaire about the 'writer's necessary engagement with the age in which he lives' by saying that it is a writer's duty to show man his image *'sub specie aeternitatis'* [in the sight of eternity] and talked about his engagement with 'what is constant in man's nature'.

HELEN: Ah yes! This is what makes me feel so uneasy. He's always going on about 'evil in men's hearts' but he never sees it in a social context or considers whether a particular kind of society develops people's potential for evil – or good. He just assumes humanity is destructive.

CONNIE: You seem to be asking him to write traditional novels.

HELEN: If by 'traditional' you mean social, realistic novels, then yes. After all, people are social beings. It would give a more balanced view than this 'transcendental evil' he's always trying to evoke.

THEO: But Angus Wilson [a contemporary English novelist] says that the disadvantage of the well-observed sociological novel is that it attempts to 'build up a citadel which will protect us'.

CONNIE: Yes, when I'm reading Golding I get that feeling of being exposed to things we usually shelter ourselves from. 'A book must be the axe that smashes the frozen sea within us' – that's Kafka [twentieth-century Czech novelist]. I don't think you get that kind of experience (I know there are exceptions) in the social novel. Instead of showing what's merely contemporary or social, Golding gets away from inessentials and focuses on 'what man is' (his words).

THEO: In 'A Moving Target' (*A Moving Target*, 166) he says he could have chosen the gasworks chimney instead of the spire. Would that have made it a social realism novel?

HELEN: Not necessarily. Does he say why he didn't use the gasworks?

THEO: It's a bit vague I think . . .

CONNIE: No, it isn't. And at last I can get in my point about Good as well as Evil. He says that when Jocelin is dying he sees 'the spire in all its glory' and that if the reader doesn't understand 'a man is overthrown by the descent into his world of beauty's mystery and irradiation, flame, explosion, then the book has failed' (*A Moving Target*, 167).

HELEN: I rather like that – especially that ambiguous 'overthrown'.

CONNIE: Yes, I'm glad there's ambiguity, even while Golding claims 'the book is as simple as a book well could be'. In Jocelin's final vision of it, the spire is 'like an upward waterfall', but it's also slim as a girl', so that even in the middle of the rapturous description of its beauty, we are reminded of the other images we've associated it with all through. That's why the spire with the pit beneath is such a powerful image of how inseparable good and evil are. (Difficult to do with gasworks!). The imagery, the story, the psychology all work together to demonstrate how it's all fused together. It's not abstract – everybody's experienced something like it. You have some brilliant idea or do something creative or daring or altruistic and then when it turns out to be more complicated than you'd thought you begin to wonder 'What made me do that?' Then if you begin to disinter all sorts of self-centred motives, it's rather frightening. If it were on a big scale – something public and you'd devoted your life to it – it would be completely undermining, especially if it had involved exploiting other people. And yet it might be an achievement too. Golding talks of the wickedness the job 'forced on' Jocelin in the same paragraph as the comments on beauty (*A Moving Target*, 167). Golding makes me understand – no, experience very intensely – things like ambition, joy, ruthlessness, wonder, self-disgust and how they're all mixed up together. I know it's platitudinous and you're laughing at me, but it's true all the same.

3.3 REASON AND VISION

THEO: No, I agree with you. I think the ending, especially, repudiates a clear-cut classification of things into good and evil. This is why he always stresses the inadequacies of reason. In 'The Ladder and the Tree' (*The Hot Gates*, 172) he says that science 'leaves no place in its exquisitely logical universe for the terrors of darkness'.

CONNIE: And in *The Spire* he's saying it leaves no place for inexplicable beauty either. What's wrong with reason is its claim to explain the universe.

HELEN: But it doesn't! He's really put up a straw man to knock down! And he almost admits it. There was a radio programme [Radio 3, December 1983] where he said that at the centre of a black hole the laws of nature no longer apply, and so physicists believe in miracles inside black holes, whereas theologians believe in them outside. It's an admission that science doesn't offer a totally explicable universe, but it's come a bit late in the day.

CONNIE: Well, I don't know what his theory was when he wrote *The Spire* but he did capture the tremendous tension between the man using reason and the man relying on vision. Roger tries to dig in his heels all the way, keeps anticipating disaster, but he responds to the challenge of Jocelin's vision and finds ways of overcoming the practical problems. The spire survives in spite of his conclusions. It ought not to, but it does – there's no explanation for it.

HELEN: Except that there probably is a rational explanation of the spire standing – I mean the one made of stone, not the one made of words. I believe some kind of very firm rock has been discovered under the marsh. All right – I know Golding's not writing a book on

that's not what its about

medieval architecture - but it does make his high evaluation of vision above reason questionable. By making his cathedral float on the marsh he's given himself such an easy hypothesis in favour of miracles.

CONNIE: If we're going to bring Salisbury Cathedral into it - and I should have thought we could only use it as something that stimulated Golding's imagination - then the fact that <u>now we know there's firm rock underneath</u> is neither here nor there. <u>The point is that people achieve marvellous things by taking risks, doing what is irrational. We limit ourselves if we only do what is explicable.</u>

3.4 PSYCHOLOGY

THEO: I wonder if this is why Golding doesn't like psychology - because he thinks it purports to *explain* human beings?

HELEN: I once went to a lecture by a psychiatrist on *The Spire*. It was hilarious - all about surrogate parents. The whole argument depended on the spire falling down at the end, symbolising, she said, Jocelin's failure to have an erection. When I pointed out that the spire doesn't fall down, she said, 'It's going to'. She didn't know what I meant when I said you've only got the words on the page.

THEO: It sounds a bit grotesque, but Jocelin's psychology is central, isn't it? Especially his sexual psychology.

HELEN: Oh yes! I'm just suggesting that the lecturer was bending the book to fit her theories, but of course it's full of sex (Golding once - as a joke - suggested *An Erection at Barchester* as a title) and it's all horrible and disgusting as always in Golding; there's no such thing as good sexual love in any of his books. He uses it as a recurrent image for the 'moral disease' he thinks humanity suffers from.

THEO: Yes, he takes a biblical line on this, doesn't he? I mean that one of the main things about the Fall was that sexuality became shameful.

CONNIE: It may be as simple as that in *The Inheritors* where the Old People are Man before the Fall, and they have some kind of lovely, gentle group sex, and the New People - who are us, *homo sapiens* - have nasty violent, lascivious sex. I think it's a bit more complicated in *The Spire* though.

3.5 CHARACTERISATION

Jocelin

HELEN: I don't see that. Jocelin is presented as suffering from sexual frustration and it's not done particularly sympathetically. He sees his wet dreams as the torments of Satan and there's nothing in the text to counteract that. He sees his love for Goody as 'prurient' and the text supports this, he even tried to ensure, by marrying her to Pangall, that if she can't have sex with him, she won't have it with anybody. Forcing up the spire is simple sublimation. Golding probably read one beginner's book on psychology.

CONNIE: This is just what I said at first – as soon as you start interpreting a book, you risk reducing it to nothing. What you've said is true, but it's misleading because in the novel it's not formulated in a clear simple statement like that. We only gradually realise that Jocelin's interest in Goody is 'prurient', and then we become aware that he, too, is gradually understanding this, so that he eventually admits the reason for arranging the marriage to Pangall. It's a subtle psychological process we watch, not a bare statement of symptoms. And then think of that moment when he decides to use Goody to keep Roger at work – that's psychologically very interesting, isn't it? All those devices to keep her virginal and then he sacrifices her virginity for the sake of the spire! And since he identifies himself with the spire . . .

HELEN: Well, yes, I could agree that . . .

CONNIE AND THEO: What? (Laughter)

HELEN: . . . and even offer you the dumb man as another complication.

CONNIE: How do you mean?

HELEN: Well, Jocelin's obviously bisexual.

CONNIE AND THEO: ? ?

HELEN: Oh come on! He's in love with the sculptor for a start. He dreams of Goody with her red hair 'humming from an empty mouth'.

THEO: Kinkead-Weekes and Gregor in *William Golding* say that it's because he wants Goody for sex and the dumb man because of his dog-like devotion.

HELEN: Really? But I thought Golding was making it absolutely clear. Jocelin doesn't want to go into heaven unless he can have her on one side and him on the other. And there's some very emotional hugging. Isn't his youthful enthusiasm for Anselm intended to suggest similar feelings? And look how he likes to feel he has a special relationship with the workmen.

CONNIE: You may be right, though I'm not sure that Joceline ever recognises that those feelings are sexual in the way he does about Goody.

THEO: Golding said he didn't know anything about homosexuality, but that it is 'built in to our society' that in a heterosexual relationship there will be exploitation of one person by another. He thought it possible that there could be a homosexual relationship without exploitation. What's sinful, he said, is 'the exploitation not the sex' [J. I. Biles, *Conversation with William Golding*].

HELEN: That's interesting. Practically the only person Jocelin doesn't exploit is the dumb man.

CONNIE: But the thing that's essentially important about the psychology of Jocelin is the way he develops. As the spire goes up, his gaze turns upward more and more (do you remember the difficulty Roger had persuading him to look down?): he repeatedly identifies himself with God. Round his feet are people begging for attention or revealing corrupt dealings – Ivo's canonisation, the aunt's influence in high places. Beneath his feet, there's the pit with its reminders of death and hell, and then Pangall buried there. Jocelin becomes more and more demented as the repressed guilt accumulates.

THEO: Yes, and yet it is presented in medieval terms, as demons and witchcraft, not in terms of a disturbed psyche.

CONNIE: And that does two things – it creates a sense of the period and it enables Jocelin to externalise his guilt. You could say the demons do for Jocelin what the 'beast' does for the boys in *Lord of the Flies*. Also, of course, he's put all his energy into getting the work completed. Once it's finished, it's possible for him to collapse.

THEO: How well I know the feeling!

HELEN: You don't think the discovery that the pillars are hollow, followed immediately by the collapse of Jocelin's spine is too obviously allegorical?

CONNIE: It might be if it stopped there but it's part of the process of Jocelin's self-discovery which gains momentum in the three final chapters. By making him question his own motives, Golding makes the connection between Jocelin's individual psyche and more general philosphical problems especially clear. He says, 'There is no innocent work' and 'God knows where God may be'.

HELEN: Platitudes! It's too explanatory.

THEO: Do you prefer, 'If I could go back, I would take God as lying between people and to be found there'?

HELEN: That's interesting but it's certainly not what the book's about. Do you think Golding is thinking about the kind of book he'd write if *he* 'could go back'?

THEO: What do you mean?

HELEN: Well, *The Spire*'s about abstract ideas, isn't it? – faith and reason and so on. The characters are just vehicles for Golding's ideas.

CONNIE: Oh how can you say that? You've already agreed that Jocelin is psychologically complex –

HELEN: No.

CONNIE: – well sexually anyway. And then look at the way he develops after the completion of the spire. He really becomes quite perceptive. He notices the water in Alison's eyes (without realising it's tears of pity though), the 'delicate calligraphy' of Father Adam's face, the beauty of the kingfisher and the appletree . . .

THEO: . . . bearing the fruit of all our woe . . .

CONNIE: – yes but angel-blossoms too. So he's changed from his single-minded obsession with getting the spire up to a realisation that the world is beautiful, and human beings too – Father Adam, anyway.

HELEN: Hang on! He sees human beings as a framework of bones covered with parchment – you can't get much more reductive than that.

CONNIE: But the way his mind oscillates – that's so interesting. After all the exploitation and the guilt, there really is something beautiful after all – the 'upward waterfall'.

HELEN: Obvous symbolism again!

CONNIE: But it is so good because it is so odd and impossible.

THEO: In spite of the Fall we can still go heavenwards.

HELEN: Oh Theo! Even Golding isn't as corny as that! And he's managed a nicely ambiguous ending – absolution under false pretences?

THEO: You mean because Father Adam misinterprets 'It's like the appletree' as 'God! God! God!'? But as a priest giving the last rites he has access to God's charity.

CONNIE: I think Helen's right. The uncertainty is in keeping with the whole complex treatment of Jocelin.

Other characters

HELEN: All right, I'll concede that there's some psychological complexity in the treatment of Jocelin, though when I'm reading, I'm fare more conscious of him as an expression of Golding's ideas than as a fully imagined human-being. But you're not going to defend the other characters on the same grounds, are you?

CONNIE: Not on the same grounds. After all, we see what Jocelin sees.

HELEN: I grant Golding's very cunning at finding a form which conceals his weaknesses. Choose as your centre of consciousness a character who has no understanding of human relationships and you free yourself at a stroke from having to bother with them.

Roger

THEO: Actually, the personal relationship between Jocelin and Roger is as interesting as the theoretical one we were talking about just now. The contrasts between them are physical – Roger's short and heavy, Jocelin tall and thin; Roger's afraid of heights, Jocelin's exhilarated by them; Roger drinks and fornicates, Jocelin is ascetic and represses his desires.

HELEN: I like the bit where Jocelin thinks that Roger and Rachel seem more like brother and sister than man and wife. At first it seems odd that he should be so perceptive and then you realise that somebody so sex-obsessed as he is might well be sensitive to such things.

CONNIE: Jocelin's sensitivity towards him while using him as a tool is very plausible – do you remember Browning – 'the honest thief, the tender murderer'? [the poem 'Fra Lippo Lippi']

HELEN: You see, we're back at Jocelin!

Goody

CONNIE: So we are! And I'm afraid Goody isn't much more than red hair and a green cloak.

THEO: She also represents a good woman – at least in medieval terms. Her modesty and submissiveness form a contrast with Alison and Rachel – at least, until her adulterous relationship with Roger.

HELEN: I've got a theory – she's subnormal. Jocelin sees her with her mouth hanging open and thinks she'd look foolish 'if anything so sweet could ever look foolish'.

Rachel

CONNIE: Are you going to polish off Rachel in one sentence too? An aspect of Golding's sexist attitude to women perhaps?

HELEN: No. I think she's really rather good. The way she starts painting her face to get her husband back is quite moving. Even Jocelin eventually recognises that her incessant talking is an expression of pain. She's one of the really good characters – she fetches Father Adam to rescue Jocelin when he's been attacked in the town.

THEO: Goodness! I'd seen her as a typical gossiping, boring female.

HELEN: Then you're certainly more sexist than Golding is.

Pangall

THEO: Sorry! I just meant boring talker. But don't you think the most important minor character is Pangall?

HELEN: No.

CONNIE: Why?

THEO: Because he's the counterpart to Jocelin. They're both scape-goats. The workmen taunt him but say he brings luck. He's a human sacrifice, buried in the foundations to make them safe.

CONNIE: But Jocelin isn't.

THEO: His heads are. And when he goes up the spire and tries to help, the workmen accept him, not because he's any real use, but because, like Pangall, he brings luck. Pangall's family have been vergers since the cathedral was first built. The grandfather saved it when unseasoned wood caught fire. He represents Christianity as opposed to the pagan workmen. That's why he's killed with mistletoe - a ritual, Druidic killing. Similarly, Jocelin is attacked in the town when he ceases to be a lucky mascot.

CONNIE: Where did you find all this?

THEO: Oh, the mistletoe reminded me of 'Balder Dead' [poem by Matthew Arnold] and that led me to Frazer's *Golden Bough* (about ancient myths) and so on.

HELEN: It's awfully interesting but it doesn't make Pangall into a person.

CONNIE: No - only in that first scene where he tries to persuade Jocelin that he really is in danger. But I think there is enough sense of humanity created for one to feel dismay when Jocelin persists in regarding him and the others as tools, and in seeing them as pillars supporting his spire.

HELEN: See - you *do* think it's a diagram.

CONNIE: But not *only* a diagram. I'd argue that Jocelin sees only caricatures of people, but then the caricature is brought to life in the novel.

Father Adam

CONNIE: Father Adam is at first 'anonymous' and then his kindliness, concern, understanding gradually impinge on Jocelin's mind.

Anselm

CONNIE: But he seems to have understood Anselm, perhaps because there's so little there to understand. His perception of the long-suffering dignity as a façade for emptiness is confirmed by the Visitor's satirical references to the man who was concerned about the candle-money. All the same, Jocelin thinking 'I must erase him' is chilling to say the least.

The workmen

CONNIE: Even the workmen have vitality. We can visualise them, and hear them. Yes, the minor characters do have life - minimal but sufficient.

3.6 MEDIEVAL ELEMENTS

THEO: We haven't considered it as a historical novel.

HELEN: Because it isn't.

THEO: Not a wholly successful one, I agree, though I can't go along with that American medieval scholar [R.C. Sutherland in J.I. Biles (ed.) *Studies in the Literary Imagination*] who attacks *The Spire* because it merely appears to be medieval but is really universal.

HELEN: How odd!

THEO: Yes. He complains that Golding hasn't done his research properly.

HELEN: So what!

CONNIE: It's a novel, not a thesis.

THEO: Apparently the theology and the church services are wrong but what's worse is the sex. He says it's post-Freudian and 'dark' instead of nice, jolly medieval sex - and there's far too much of it. I was rather shattered when I first read it because I'd felt *The Spire* had a plausibly medieval 'feel' to it. The descriptions of the building work seem to me to be especially vividly imagined. I don't think anybody knows exactly how they did it. I should think studying the building itself, as Golding did, was as good a way as any of imagining what it was like to be there at the time. For instance, when I was at Salisbury last summer, I saw an effigy of the first person to be buried in the cathedral - he was the Earl of Salisbury. This was in the thirteenth century, so the effigy was there when the work on the spire was started. There's a notice on the tomb - I've got it with my notes - here it is: 'It was discovered that the effigy had been painted twice in medieval times with what could be a layer of builder's dust between the two layers of paint'. I feel pretty sure that notice was the source of the descriptions in *The Spire* of the dust floating thick in the sunlight, the men working with cloths over their mouths, and, of course, the dung-coloured effigies - perhaps even of that whole scene with Anselm reproachfully coughing. That seems to be a real use of an historical imagination and far more important than knowing whether mattins was at 4 or 6 a.m.

HELEN: I couldn't agree more.

CONNIE: Of course, it isn't *just* medieval. There's Stonehenge. That sense of Christianity and paganism coexisting is interesting. The Christians feel really frightened and threatened by it, I suppose because their religion is still fairly new. It's almost as if Stonehenge is a rival cathedral just beyond the rim of the downs. The pagan workers kill Pangall, but working on the Christian building causes deaths too. He could have used Stonehenge as the centre of the book and called it *The Stones* instead of *The Spire*.

3.7   MODERN IMPLICATIONS

HELEN: That gives it an enormous timespan – from Stonehenge to now.

CONNIE: Yes. I wonder if Golding saw a parallel between Jocelin and the people at Los Alamos during the war, working frantically to get the atom bomb before Hitler did and seeing it as saving humanity.

THEO: And then realising what they'd done. Yes. Some of them would probably echo Jocelin's words now: 'I thought I was doing a great work; and all I was doing was bringing ruin and breeding hate'.

HELEN: You couldn't treat the bomb directly. Not in a novel.

CONNIE: No. But *The Spire is* about space. There's a lot about being up so high, where no human being has ever been before. Jocelin finds it very exciting – for all the complicated reasons we've been talking about; he's getting his erection up, he can 'oversee' everything, he's like God up there, and he enjoys the sheer physical exhilaration of height and risk. I imagine spacemen would share at least some of those feelings.

THEO: Yes, Golding certainly had space exploration in mind – he says so in 'An Affection for Cathedrals' (*A Moving Target*, 17); he calls the spire 'a technological gamble which makes space travel seem child's play'. And there's a bit in 'Egypt from my Outside' (*A Moving Target*, 58) which is even more relevant: 'Granted the illogicality of spending all that money on moonwalks – and I don't grant it . . . Without idiotic wastefulness we should not have all our palaces and gardens and tiny jewelled fragments of the moon for our enjoyment'.

HELEN: He's being ironical, I presume.

THEO: I'm not sure . . .

CONNIE: I heard a programme about the space shuttle last night –

HELEN: I thought you spent the whole night on your paper!

CONNIE: – I was just making some coffee – anyway, it proved extremely useful and got me going again when I was stuck. One of the researchers said that of course, as with any vehicle, accidents were inevitable and lives would be 'shed'. He said he hoped people would be 'mature enough' to accept this and not let it interfere with the space programme.

HELEN: 'Shed' is good! Like leaves drifting off the trees! Jocelin was more honest, admitting the cost.

CONNIE: Yes, you're right there; but he has a similar air of detachment when one of the workmen falls to his death at the crossways; and when that man's arm is burnt, he merely thinks 'there were plenty of people about to look after him if they chose to'.

THEO: All the same, Golding's not saying people shouldn't take risks. But when I went up the tower at Salisbury and saw the smoke from Porton [the chemical warfare research station] rising over the downs, I felt the same sort of chill Jocelin must have felt when he saw the smoke rising from the 'bale-fires' of the devil-worshippers.

CONNIE: And that reminds us that there's lots of religious fanaticism about, now as then, causing people to be exploited, killed . . .

THEO: It seems a bit trivial to mention money after all this.

HELEN: I meant *human* cost just now, of course.

THEO: I know. But in fact there's quite a lot in the book about the financial cost, too, about Jocelin getting the money by disreputable means and also building up enormous debts, and causing dissension in the Chapter. It's just the same now. They need millions to repair the spire before it collapses. The 'voluntary' charge for entry has outraged some people. There's a proposal to raise money by having a car park in the Close. They're not only quarrelling about whether to have it at all, but also where to have it, since nobody wants it in front of his own house. And so on.

HELEN: Timeless, isn't it?

THEO: Help, no! We're missing the Malory lecture.

CONNIE: Damn! Where's my notebook? Aren't you coming?

HELEN: No, I think I'll finish *Darkness Visible* instead.

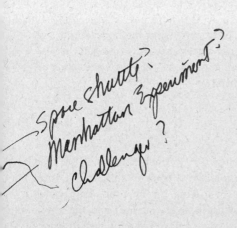

4 TECHNIQUE

4.1 CONCENTRATION

'The act of creation is a fierce, concentrated light that plays on a small area' (Moving Target, 146).

This sentence from 'Rough Magic' captures the essence of Golding's novels, and, in particular, of *The Spire*. Some critics have suggested that he works within such narrow limits that the novels are cramping, even claustophobic. Others find that the intensity of concentration creates a work of great power. Is your own experience of reading the novel one of restriction and confinement? Or does it stimulate and extend your imagination?

The setting is a restricted one, a cathedral and its immediate surroundings in a small town. The time-span is short, a couple of years in the fourteenth century. There are very few characters, and only one is developed in depth. 'Concentrated' and 'restricted' seem apt words. This chapter will examine the techniques which Golding uses to achieve fierceness of concentration, and will consider what are the other effects of his methods. An intense and concentrated work of art is not necessarily self-contained; it may create a sense of expansion, of opening doors on the universe in spite of, or even because of the 'fierce concentration on a limited area'.

4.2 STRUCTURE

The sense of a tight structure is mainly due to the centrality of the spire and to the strongly visual way in which we perceive this. It is a focal point, drawing everything towards itself, from Jocelin continually gazing at it, the workers working on it, townspeople staring at it and the travellers and roads redirecting their paths towards it, to the more distant barges bringing stone from Purbeck and the Visitor with the Holy Nail gradually approaching from as far away as Rome. Its position in a hollow with a 'rim' of downs around it emphasises that it is the centre of a circle, and the rim becomes 'the rim of the world'. Beyond it is Stonehenge with its pagan rites. The new cathedral peers at the old one over the rim of the downs. The cathedral services are in disarray but the pagan midsummer rites persist. This hints at a world not dominated by the spire. In contrast to the spire's centripetal attraction there is the centrifugal movement as the workers down tools and go off to the bale-fires which Jocelin sees round the horizon. Even his sense of the spire as the architectural centre turns out to be a simplified view. The aspiring spire has another direction; it is 'an arrow shot into the ground'. It moves upwards into space or heaven, and downwards into the earth or hell. The physical world becomes metaphysical, or – since that hell is the human mind – psychological. So the spire, with its foundations in the pit, may be made out of stone or faith or sin. It began as a diagram, then became a phallus and eventually a building. All the time it is a human being. All the main characters are 'built-in' in various ways. Jocelin's heads are literally built into both pit and spire. (Virtually everything in the novel is both factual and metaphorical).

In these ways – and many others – the novel has multiple dimensions. Talking generally about 'what man is for' Golding stressed both 'the need to have a sense of discrete, disparate phenomena at every level' and also of the 'overriding necessity' to 'bring the whole thing together'. He insisted on the unity of all kinds of events, psychological, emotional, religious and so on and 'even fetching the milk in in the morning'. This perception of unity is reflected in the structure of his novels, perhaps especially in *The Spire*; there is a multiplicity of elements, most of them moving towards, converging on the spire, and even those that are not exist only in their opposition to it.

This rigorous concentration is intensified by the paring away of all extraneous material. Golding's first plans for the novel contained much more detail about Jocelin's earlier life, which in the finished novel is given in an extremely elliptical form. It is possible to envisage the novel with a much fuller picture of the life of the townspeople, or with some individuality given to the workmen. The danger of eliminating so much is that the structure of the novel may become diagrammatic. Golding highlights the problem by making the central character a pattern-maker who learns painfully the falsity of diagrams. Jocelin uses windows as a framing device to give 'definition and importance' to the building. He repeatedly thinks he has achieved that unity of vision that Golding sees as so important. Even when the hollowness of the pillars was shown to him, 'then all things came together' and he threw himself down on the stones of the crossways, physically and spiritually, to destroy himself. But, of course, his interpretation is wrong, everything has not 'come together'. This episode parallels the previous occasion when he threw himself down at the crossways in ectasy at his unifying, simplifying vision of the spire. The image of the horrific, proliferating, plant with anguished faces entangled in its branches refutes both the destructive and the ecstatic vision. On the last page, the spire is again framed by a window and Golding finally brings the conflicting elements together with the image of the upward waterfall. This evokes the response from Jocelin, ' "Now - I know nothing at all" ', thus undercutting any confidence in a clear or perfected pattern that the image might have suggested.

The treatment of the ending of this kind of novel is particularly important. Golding was the first to use the word 'gimmick' for the sudden change of viewpoint at the end which characterises his first three works. In *The Spire* the ending is more subtle, more complicated, more enigmatic, whether you place the shift at the arrival of the Visitor or in the last three lines of the book. It is characteristic of this novel that it combines the finality of the death of the central character (one of the traditional ways of 'rounding off' a novel) with something of the uncertainty and ambiguity of an open ending.

Do you think too much has been pared away in *The Spire*? Does the patterning give the impression of existence as controllable, or at least explicable? Is such shaping desirable in a work of art?

4.3 POINT OF VIEW

The structure of *The Spire* is, of course, governed by the use of Jocelin as a centre of consciousness. It sets limits, narrows the focus, shapes the whole novel. (See Chapter 2 for a detailed account of the initial effects of using Jocelin in this way.) As we saw in the first chapter, there is the extraordinarily vivid sense of being inside Jocelin's mind while simultaneously we are repeatedly invited to criticise it. As we explore more deeply we may become, paradoxically, both more sympathetic because of the mental anguish we are forced to share and comprehend and also more appalled because of the ruthlessness with which he forces through his plans. The evocation of such contradictory impulses is a good illustration of how an apparently restricting and controlled form can open out. Similarly, by choosing as central character one who moves from dazzling certainty through tormenting uncertainty to an acknowledgement of knowing nothing Golding has built tentativeness into the structure.

Does the unreliability of Jocelin as narrator create unnecessary difficulties? There certainly are some difficulties. His repression of his knowledge about Pangall - both of his impotence and of his death -

leaves the reader also wondering 'where is Pangall?' But such mysteries are essential to the novel. Without them there would be no suspense and no exploration of subconscious motives. The deeper we go into Jocelin's mind, the more unreliable he is bound to become. The incoherence and mental chaos of Chapter 8 can be experienced with such immediacy because of Golding's methods of articulating the different levels of Jocelin's consciousness. Though we become immersed in his view of things, we do not become committed to it.

4.4 NARRATIVE TECHNIQUE

As far as the unravelling of the story is concerned, *The Spire* is a traditional linear narrative, moving through a period of about two years in a straightforward way, pin-pointing the passage of time by reference to the weather, the seasons and sometimes the month. There are a few deviations from this steady progression through time – the occasional flashbacks when Jocelin remembers episodes from his past, the time by the sea with Anselm, Goody as a child, the arranged marriage and the more extended incursion of the past into the present with the reading of his account of his vision. The withholding of information (not only about Pangall's death, but about Goody's pregnancy, the state of the cathedral finances and all those details which Anselm reveals in his last meeting with Jocelin) is a technique especially associated with the detective story, but it is a common way in any narrative of arousing curiosity and holding attention.

The linear movement forms a complete contrast to the ambiguity and complexity of the total experience presented by the novel, which is so packed and concentrated that we cannot be sure that we have grasped its implications. The flashes of light and darkness intermittently show scenes of great clarity but reveal no certainty about the whole. Jocelin's continual repression of knowledge about himself and others leaves us groping for explanations. The state of the church and the disarray of the Chapter are hazy because Jocelin will not look at these things. The chronological movement through time is an important element because it suggests simplicity only to reveal how delusory such expectations are.

4.5 IMAGERY

The imagery in *The Spire* forms an intricate and complex pattern. The details of individual images are significant, but even more important, a network of images creates a pattern, shaping the whole structure of the

novel. They form groups or series. There is one which suggests height,
heaven and aspiration; this includes birds, angels, light, fire, and of course
the spire itself, with which they are all linked. Opposed to these is a
group suggesting depth, hell and destruction; darkness, the pit, the cellarage
and water function in this way. But the 'high' images don't stay up on the
heights; the angel turns into a devil, the eagle turns out to be a raven,
(in folklore a harbinger of death) and most of all the spire has its foundations in the pit. Between these two levels come, naturally, the earth
images: trees and plants with their roots in the earth but growing towards
the sun, and the Cathedral itself, frequently seen as a human body lying
on the earth. Since it is built on a marsh, the notion of the human being
swiftly sinking into the depths is always present. The cathedral as a ship
suggests that it, too, is floating precariously just above hell-mouth.

Trees and plants
The trees and plants connect the ground with heaven and hell. The
strangling, contorted plant is a disturbing image, suggesting evil sprouting
and proliferating from the earth – or from Jocelin. It grows in his mind. As
Father Adam tries to make him see his old vision in a new light, he struggles
to 'escape from something so deep, it must lie close to the root of the
plant'. This metaphorical plant is also the mistletoe. Every mention of
the mistletoe is in terms of horror and the word 'obscene' recurs several
times. (The Druids' idea that the berries were the semen of the gods may
well contribute to Jocelin's revulsion.) The 'riotous confusion of its branches'
is alarming as is Jocelin's disgust at the berry on his shoe. At the inquiry,
'mistletoe' evokes a question 'as hard and sharp as the edge of a stone';
the commission sits motionless, intent, looking at him as if he were on
trial. Golding weaves the mistletoe as a pagan symbol into naturalistic
treatment of it as sign of a physical threat to the spire. Mistletoe grows
on living oak trees. If the wood used in the building were unseasoned, it
could continue to grow; this would be a sign that there was an actual,
scientifically explicable danger. This interrelationship of the actual and
the symbolic is very important. Symbolism which becomes almost totally
abstract, existing for its symbolic significance only, tends to make little
emotional impact; it leads to a purely intellectual recognition of the parallels the writer is indicating.

Compare the treatment of the mistletoe with that of the devils. Do you
find the devils as disturbing as the episodes of the mistletoe? Are you more
moved when the scaly-winged devils clamour at the windows or when
Goody and her friends turn into little devils?

Similarly, the appletree makes its impact not so much because we
associate it with the Garden of Eden and the Fall but because it is for the
reader as well as Jocelin a sudden unexpected sight of actual beauty –

exciting and dazzling. He sees it at the same time as the flash of the king-fisher, a bird whose flight is so swift that a momentary glimpse of colour – 'all the blue of the sky condensed to a winged sapphire' – is all that one can see. The apple blossom is a cloud of angels, the kingfisher 'condenses' the sky but it is the sensuous experience – the sight and smell – that is so vivid. The symbolic implications are all the more striking because of this. It is Jocelin's first recognition of beauty, his first glimpse of something heavenly in earthly things and the beginning of an awareness of the com-plexities of life as he notices the 'long black springing thing' and realises that 'there is more to the appletree than one branch'. This recognition of the complex beauty of the tree contrasts with the simplicity of his 'original diagram' of the spire. It also contrasts with the threatening com-plexities of the strangling plant with tortured faces in it; and this plant is what the spire became in Jocelin's imagination when he saw the mistletoe.

It is possible to pursue the pattern further by noting all the other tree images. The spire is a tree, at first excitingly high, making Jocelin feel like a small boy who has climbed too high, and later terrifyingly high when it sways in the wind. The pillar with the scaffolding round it looks like a fir tree, there is a 'grove' of pinnacles at the corners of the Tower, the dust creates 'trunks' of sunlight. To accumulate such lists of examples is to run the risk of playing hunt the symbol. With many books, doing this might well be forcing a pattern on what are really casual connections. Here, though, the pattern is so intricate and so much of the essence of the book that I would hesitate to dismiss any image as a mere chance occurrence. All the main images reinforce what is being said in other ways, through story, dialogue, characterisation, articulation of thoughts. They all ramify and intertwine. Like everything else in the book, they direct us towards some aspect of the spire.

Up and down

The spire pointing heavenwards with the pit beneath it might seem to offer the simple equation, up equals good, down equals bad. This is not so, as the spire's tendency to turn into a destructive plant shows. It is also threatening when it is a club, a stone hammer, a phallus. That it is frightening when it is phallic is in keeping with the treatment, throughout the novel, of sexuality as alarming or disgusting. The use of the detachable spire of the model to taunt Pangall makes it a bawdy joke. It is also taken out by Jocelin, who studies it minutely, nurses it lovingly as if it were a baby, clutches it so tightly that the point grinds into his cheek. In his sleep, his repressed sexual fears come to the surface; he dreams that 'everybody knew the church had no spire, nor could have any' and they taunt him as Pangall was taunted. Only Satan can erect this phallic spire.

Roger, on the other hand treats it with casual familiarity, 'Fall when you like, me old cock'.

It is also 'a diagram of prayer', as well as a building which we have watched being built in all its complicated detail – and not only watched, but heard, and smelled, staggered under the weight of it. In these ways, without abstractions or putting it in conceptual terms, Golding combines in a single unified image the spiritual, the instinctual and the physical.

The pit

The pit from one angle, is simply a hole in the earth, whose physical features are examined minutely. It stinks – literally, because of the decomposing bodies buried under the cathedral. The repeated references to the stench and to the disgust seen on the faces of the people in the vicinity are characteristic of the sensuousness of Golding's writing; whether the sense-experience is loathsome or enjoyable, it is always vivid. The physical repulsion and the actuality of the decaying bodies of 'noseless men' give the idea of hell and 'the damned stirring' a horrifying immediacy. The actual pit and the symbolic hell are completely integrated.

It is also a grave 'for some notable' and 'a pit to catch a dean'. It was on this spot, 'here where the pit stinks' that Jocelin had this original vision. Vision and corruption start from the same place. The human complications of the pit are psychological. It represents the aspects of Jocelin's psyche which he tries to keep hidden from himself. It exactly matches (though I suppose Golding would not like the term) the id, Sigmund Freud's name for the part of the mind whose existence we do not want to admit and whose contents we can only glimpse. It is here that Jocelin feels he has buried his repressed desires and his guilty knowledge. His anger rises out of 'some pit' inside him. His knowledge about Pangall is 'down in the vaults, the cellarage of my mind', which he later calls 'the cellarage where the rats live'. After the vision of the appletree, he begins to understand the connections: 'What's a man's mind? Is it the whole building, cellarage and all?'

The whole building

In asking these questions, Jocelin is bringing together the whole range of images and expressing their implications in both conceptual and symbolic terms. By calling the pit a cellar (of a particularly terrifying kind for those who have read 'The Ladder and the Tree') he highlights its integral relation with the rest of the building and with himself. This links up with his feeling that he is carrying the whole weight on his spine. This was welcome at first and interpreted as an Angel warming his back and encouraging him in his enterprise. The change to the devil kicking him parallels the gradual emergence into consciousness of his evil motives, previously buried in the pit. There is a corresponding physical deterioration as the tuberculosis progresses and as the spire sways, bends and starts to crumble. He says, 'My spire pierced every stage from bottom to top', thus emphasising the analogy with the spine which carries the whole central nervous system.

In these ways, Golding uses symbol and imagery to convey how completely Jocelin is 'built in'. Father Adam makes it (perhaps unnecessarily) explicit when he says 'life is a rickety building'. On the other hand, by offering the possibility of spiritual or psychological or medical interpretations of what is happening, Golding leaves the explanation open.

Angels, devils, birds and other winged creatures

The angel – devil symbolism makes it clear that Jocelin is as much an image-maker as his creator, so that images seem to arise directly from his psychological state. By interpreting the warmth at his back as divine support he bolsters up his confidence in his project. He uses birds in a similar way. He persists in identifying a great bird floating at the tower-top as an eagle, even as St John's eagle (Revelation 4.7), one of the 'beasts' round the throne of God, although the dumb man knows that he has got it wrong. Just as the good angel has its opposite in the bad angel or devil, so the eagle has its opposite in the raven (black, and in folklore a harbinger of death). It is also just a bird, 'sane and daylight and matter of fact'. Jocelin sees himself as an eagle, but he perches on the wall of the tower 'like a raven on the edge of a cliff', and Alison describes him as 'a great bird hunched in the rain'. He recognises eventually that he cannot take off and soar among eagles, that he is human and earthbound, like an old crow 'inching along' to see Roger. Even here, though, he still clings to the idea of a winged being, albeit a decrepit one.

There are birds inside the building as well as outside. The swallow, which makes its nest in buildings, is a recurrent image. Pangall's 'swallow's nest' cottage and Roger's 'swallow's nest' hut are both observed from a distance by Jocelin. He perceives them both as illegal, Pangall's made of stolen material and Roger's the scene of adultery. They both have a fascination for him, both being places of unsatisfactory sexual relationships about which he has cause for guilt. These people are small birds to him. So are the workmen. The inside of the tower with the scaffolding looks as if 'very methodical birds had been building'. It is 'bare of birds' when the men are at a meeting. It is the effect of perspective that, seen from far below, they look like small birds or even seem to be 'flysize'. But it is also characteristic of Jocelin to see most people as small.

This makes his use of the mayfly as an image all the more unexpected. He assures Roger that he isn't going to use this fly which lives only for a single day as a symbol for life's brevity. He uses it instead to urge Roger into taking risks, venturing into the unknown, just as the mayfly, with its total lack of previous experience, must spend its whole life exploring the unknown. He asks him to see life differently, to dare to act without calculation and precedent. (You might consider the bearing of this on the writer or artist contemplating a new work).

Seeing

The Spire is concerned with ways of seeing. Images of seeing, of refusing to see, of failing to see, of misunderstanding what is seen, run through the whole book. Windows and lights may disclose a true picture – or not. (There is some play on the word 'light' meaning a section of a mullioned window.) Jocelin's unfocused eyes sometimes see separately. As he is dying, he sees two eyes looking at him. They slide together and become the window, but it is still divided – by the spire. The division itself becomes beautiful, 'still and silent but rushing upwards'. The tremendous tension of trying to bring everything together is suggested by images of breaking ('the substance was one thing that broke all the way to eternity') and splitting ('wild flashes of thought split the darkness') and the eyes remain 'either eye'. 'Terror and joy' come together in a chaotic mixture and the final keynote is of 'incomprehension' as Father Adam misinterprets Jocelin's last words.

There are many other patterns of imagery which could be traced. You might like to look at tents/nets/ropes/chains or arrows/spears/needles or gargoyles.

Effect of patterning

The division of this discussion on imagery into subsections is designed to clarify by separating out various images. But too much clarity falsifies the book. The images are all interrelated and they must be put back together after inspection. The effect of such intricate patterning of imagery is to create a sense of a tightly-controlled structure while, at the same time, because the pattern is so complex and proliferates as we try to examine it, to suggest that it is growing and branching uncontrollably. The tension between the desire for unity and the recognition of chaos seems to me central to the book.

*   *   *

Note on Berenice

The striking image of Goody's red hair blazing among the stars comes from a poem by the Latin poet Catullus about Berenice, who placed a lock of her hair in a shrine as a surety for the safe return of her husband from war. The lock disappeared and the Astronomer Royal discovered it in the night sky as a new constellation.

Hair blazing among stars is what reminds Jocelin of Berenice. It seems a fairly slight connection, put in merely to allow Jocelin his moment of amusement at Father Adam's innocence in thinking that he is referring to *Saint* Berenice. But there is more to the story than this. Berenice, in love with Ptolemy III, was forced by her mother into an engagement to Demetrius. He, however, was keener on the mother than the daughter; so Berenice arranged for him to be caught in her mother's bedroom and assassinated. Then she married Ptolemy. Her anxiety for his safety leads to the story of the hair. This makes the links with *The Spire* closer - an unwanted husband murdered to make another relationship possible. It suggests that Jocelin, on his deathbed, is still afraid that Goody might have been involved in the death of Pangall, in order to make her love affair with Roger easier.

This seems to me far too much to hang on to the one word 'Berenice'. The difficult and the mysterious stimulate the imagination. But by connecting the blazing hair with Berenice, Golding has reduced a vivid image to an intellectual puzzle.

* * *

4.6 LANGUAGE

It will be obvious from this 'dance of figurative language' that Golding's prose is of a highly poetic kind. It is often intense, even violent, as in the explosive opening. This is a way of projecting Jocelin's obsessive enthusiasm; he doesn't just see the spire 'springing' from the body of a man lying in the marsh, but 'springing, projecting, bursting, erupting from the heart of the building'. By the time we reach 'erupting' the spire has acquired volcanic proportions. This use of lists is effective in suggesting Jocelin's frenetic mental state. Repetition is used to similar effect in the account of the death of Goody. The repetition of 'jerked', 'scream', 'belly', 'knife', 'stabbing', 'blood' creates a lurid scene which then recurs in even more chaotic form in Jocelin's mind. Some critics take the view that this style is exaggerated and prone to purple patches. It is an extreme style, but, in my view, appropriate to the extremes of feeling Golding deals with.

Detail
Golding has another style for another kind of intensity. The passages describing the work on the building give concentrated attention to minute detail so that we, with Jocelin, watch intently. Golding is exact, without

over-using technical language, for, of course, Jocelin does not know the technical terms, but refers to 'the sighting thing' and so on. But the layman's closely observed description of the use of the T-square and the plumb-line, or the way the stonemasons create the arch above windows enables the reader to see these processes in his mind's eye. But it is not just detached observations of technique. This kind of precision conveys Jocelin's intentness as he holds his breath at a crucial moment or represses his irritation at the slowness of some procedure. The use of the schoolboy's counters on the wall of the cloister far below to measure the sway of the spire combines an almost mathematical exactness of description with a disturbing emotional effect. Looking at the game at first seems to offer 'a kind of childish security', which vanishes as the sixth counter slides into view.

Onomatopoeia (words which make the sound of the thing they signify)

This immediacy is sometimes heightened by the use of sounds. The book is full of noises, shouting, banging and so on. This is especially vivid when two senses are combined; Jocelin *sees* a whistle going round a corner, sees voices *writing*. More frequent is the use of onomatopoeic sounds. This can evoke not only the sound but the situation. When Jocelin wants to feel that the church services are insignificant, the singing sounds to him like 'wah! wah! wah!' (The repetition of 'Tap! Tap!' is an economical way of announcing the dumb sculptor's presence, but there is so much of this kind of thing that it begins to seem little more than an irritating habit on Golding's part. When the steel band round the tower says 'wangle-angle-bangle-clang' and the pillars cry 'eeeeeee' I begin to feel that I'm reading a children's story. ('The little red train went chuff, chuff, chuff and the whistle cried "eeeeeee".') Golding also uses these devices in his essays, where they are even more inappropriate. Inventive use of language can be very exciting. The cumulative effect of these recurring sounds is to suggest noises echoing round the cathedral, but some of the individual instances seem a bit silly. Check your own response by comparing a number of examples and considering what kinds of effect they create.

Coinages

Golding also uses coinages – words he has invented – such as 'uncountry' and 'notsong' to condense into a single word the notion of Jocelin existing in two worlds, the actual world and his mental world which is remote from it yet immediate to him. The compound word 'panicshot' in the phrase 'panicshot darkness' fuses a number of impressions, the explosiveness of a shot in the dark, the texture of the darkness (like shot-silk) and the rush of words coming so fast that they cannot be separated.

Archaic diction

The diction is modern, apart from a few words used to give a slightly medieval flavour. 'Mystery' is used in the medieval sense of 'craft', while retaining a suggestion of its modern meaning. 'Noisome' ('stinking' in Middle English) nicely suggests a cross between noise and stench. 'Widdershins' simply means going the wrong way but onomatopoeically and visually it evokes a picture of Jocelin rushing awkwardly on shaky shins. These seem to fit appropriately with the mainly twentieth-century language. An exception is 'beldame' for sexuality, which stands out incongruously in its strangeness. The biblical language – there are frequent quotations and references – seems entirely appropriate. The rhythmical prose of the Authorised Version blends perfectly with Golding's heightened prose.

Disjunction

One of the most interesting features of the language of *The Spire* is this intensity, expressing Jocelin's turbulent, sometimes frenzied, mental activity. Golding has developed a technique which enables him to move in and out of a character's mind without any of the usual pointers to indicate that he is doing so. In the first chapter, he uses a variety of methods in quick succession.

No, he said to himself, they can't have done it yet . . .
He whispered . . .
'It's true. After all these years . . . Glory be'. For they were doing the unthinkable. I have walked there for years, he thought . . .
Courage. Glory be . . . Like a surgeon, I take my knife . . .
And his mind played for a while with the fancy . . .

The passage starts conventionally, apart from the absence of inverted commas; presumably this is thought, not speech. Then there are some words in inverted commas – words that are voiced, in a whisper. In the next paragraph 'he thought' is the indicator that we are still following Jocelin's mental processes. In the following paragraph, syntax is discarded in the first two 'sentences' and with no intervening 'he thought' from the narrator, we seem to be sharing Jocelin's thoughts at first hand – for the moment. 'And his mind played . . .' whisks us out again and into the past tense, distanced, and dependent on the narrator for knowledge of what is going on in Jocelin's mind.

The techniques used in this passage are relatively simple, but they prepare us for the complications of Chapter 8:

What's this called? And this?
Sometimes . . . he would put propositions to himself . . .
'When it's finished I shall be free'
Or: 'It's part of the cost, you see'
Or: 'I know Anselm as a person; and him; and him.
But I never knew her. It would be so precious to me if - '
What's this called? And this?
Once . . . when I felt calm . . . He was remembering . . . another life.
There was God!

This is much more complicated and enigmatic. Try to work out what is the function of the first two uses of italics. Is the effect the same the second time? Is the third use of italics (*There was God!*) different? To whom do you think 'you see' is addressed? What is the effect of 'and him; and him'?

Using these devices, Golding can move rapidly in and out of Jocelin's mind, without any laborious announcement that he is doing so, and he can also convey the various levels of consciousness at which the mind is operating. After the broken-off sentences, the staccato words in italics come down like a shutter, barring the way into consciousness of the terrifying thoughts about Goody.

The absence of explanatory linking material between the different modes gives an almost kaleidoscopic view of Jocelin's mind. In Chapter 8, when Jocelin becomes frenzied and incoherent after the death of Goody, Golding puts words in brackets as a way of suggesting mental chaos. He is always careful to move gradually into incoherence. He tells us that 'Jocelin would find himself repeating one word endlessly, no, no, no, no, no, perhaps, or well, well, well, well,' before he starts inserting repeated phrases and words in brackets without further introduction. In these ways, Golding suggests the simultaneity of several levels of Jocelin's consciousness. The reported thoughts, in syntactically complete sentences, suggest a capacity for detached observation. The words in inverted commas, giving us direct access to his thoughts, show a feverish kind of desperate rationality. Juxtaposed to these are the words in brackets revealing the frantic mind flinching away from unbearable memories and guilt. The jerkiness of the abrupt switches from one mode to another also adds to the impression of a disordered mind.

This purposefully disjointed effect is also achieved by other means, such as abandoning the conventions of syntax, even in descriptive passages: 'Chin up, hands holding the model spire before him, eyes half closed; joy - '. Missing out the main verbs here and in sentences such as 'Joy, fire, joy' suggests an ecstatic tossing-away of the normal controls of grammar. Verbless lists - 'Nose like an eagle's beak. Mouth wide open.'

- pare the language down to bare essentials. The disjointed effect is even
greater when it is printed in a column:

I have given it my back.
Him.
Her.
Thou.

This layout increases the disjointedness. Does it have any other effects?

Golding is not an innovator in fracturing normal structures so as to get
closer to the irrational aspects of the mind. Experiments of this kind are a
common feature of the twentieth-century novel, but each has its individual
methods.

4.7 A NOVEL ABOUT WRITING A NOVEL

These, too, have become quite common of recent years. Golding does it
quite unobtrusively, since the similarities between creators of works of
art, whether buildings, books or anything else do not need stressing. The
search for form is the central preoccupation of both author and character.
At the beginning, Jocelin foresees the outcome of his enterprise, 'the
pattern of worship complete at last'. He later observes how the spire
'enforces a pattern on the landscape' but, towards the end, the pattern,
he feels, is not complete – it is just 'a formless thing in his head'. But the
novelist makes everything tumultuously come together in Jocelin's final
view of the spire as a fusion of all the main elements of the novel.

The allusions to writing at first seem merely coincidental. Jocelin sees
'words as if written in Pangall's head' – a rather surprising perception
since he is so reluctant to read letters and documents. Then he uses that
chilling verb 'erase' when he is annoyed with Anselm. These are just faint
hints of the notion that things can be controlled in terms of reading and
writing. Jocelin's interest in naming things ('What's this called? And this?')
is a way of controlling his disintegrating mind. Roger's irritated response
represents the practical mind, more concerned with using things than
recreating them in words. But Jocelin also recognises the difficulty of
expressing in words something never experienced before, 'to which no one
could put a name'. This is the dawning realisation of Jocelin and the
builders that they are up in the air where no human being has ever been
before. Golding finds an image for it; the realisation is like the sense of a
sudden drop in temperature. The difficulty of making the intangible

tangible or visible corresponds to the difficulty of embodying a vision in stone or words.

Gradually, the references to writing become more direct. Jocelin's memories are 'like sentences from a story, which, though they left great gaps, still told enough. It was a story of her and Robert and Rachel and Pangall and the men'. The metaphors of writing and language have been coalesced into a specific story, the one we are reading. Not only are the plot and characters the same, but also the style: 'the story, with disjunct sentences, burned in his head'.

Jocelin struggles always to impose his version of the story. This is explicit when he counters Roger's account of a hypothetical collapse of the spire with his own version of its daring, unreasonable and inexplicable erection. This story he attributes to 'Voice of the devouring Will, my master'. This has an interesting parallel with Golding's comments on writing in 'Rough Magic': 'For all the complexity of literature there is a single focus in literature, a point of the blazing human will'. (*A Moving Target*, 149). Of course, we must not identify Golding with Jocelin except as creators of works of art, and even here they are by no means identical. Golding's 'blazing will' suggests a fierce vitality, in contrast to the destructiveness suggested by a 'devouring' will.

The parallels between the spire and *The Spire* are developed even more explicitly in Chapter 10, where a passage from Jocelin's Vision indicates that his original concept was of the building as a vast book, with a pinnacle as the key to unlock it. (This refers to those valuable medieval books which were sometimes fitted with lock and key to protect the delicate illuminated pages from careless readers.) The image then changes to the familiar one (familiar since Chapter 1) of the cathedral as a man, and the inside becomes 'a vividly written book to instruct that man', thus fusing cathedral, man, book into a single image. Jocelin understands the 'secret language' of the builders, the cathedral is a 'manual of heaven and hell' and the centre of this book is the spire.

This is another parallel between Golding and Jocelin; each wrote an account of the project before the attempt to embody it in stone or words (*The Spire*, 191-4; *A Moving Target*, 164-6). Golding's experience as a novelist is clearly the source of much of Jocelin's experience as a creator of the spire. In describing his own creativity, he writes:

A novelist having gone down from the confusion of daily experience to the supportive multiplicity beneath it and down again to the magical area of his own intuitions will come up to the scaffolding, the supportive machinery of his story. (*A Moving Target*, 198)

Here we see how Roger fits into the creative process. After the exploration of the depths comes the calculating and structuring. Roger 'bartering weight for strength' matches the novelist paring away inessentials, achieving strength through the narrow intensity of his focus.

The argument between Jocelin and Roger about daring to go so high reflects the 'dare' of the novel. In 'Egypt from my Inside' (*The Hot Gates*, 81) Golding writes of suggesting 'mysteries with no solution' and of mixing 'the strange, the gruesome and the beautiful' and thus avoiding confining ourselves to 'the accepted potential'. To go beyond these limits is the function of art.

Novels about writing novels have become commonplace. In *The Spire*, the novel-writing analogy broadens out into an exploration of the motives and the cost of any human enterprise and of the value of daring to explore beyond accepted boundaries.

4.8 CHARACTERISATION

Jocelin, through whose consciousness the whole of the book (apart from the last three lines) is presented, clearly cannot be summed up simply under the heading of 'characterisation'. His complex and changing inner life forms the substance of the book. In addition there are the comments of the other characters on him, their attempts to argue with him, the expression on their faces at the sight of him, and the dumb man's perception, expressed in stone. The relationship between Jocelin and the spire and the pit is integral to Golding's conception.

The treatment of the other characters is necessarily slight. You may remember that in Chapter 3 of this book, one of the students said they were 'sufficient' (she didn't say sufficient for what). Did you agree with her? They are, inevitably, extremely limited since Golding presents them as seen by Jocelin and, as we are constantly made aware, he is barely conscious that other human beings have an existence apart from himself. As the work on the spire moves towards its climax he sees himself as 'part of the crew' and knows these unnamed men 'better than he had ever known anybody in his life, from the dumb man to Jehan'.

Roger
It is built into the structure of the play that all the psychological depth and complexity is centred on Jocelin. The other characters function as part of the pattern. The only one with the human capacity for development (or deterioration) is Roger. His changes are shown in a fairly indirect way as they are observed by Jocelin or reported by Rachel. He functions chiefly as a contrast to Jocelin, opposing his practicality to Jocelin's vision, but also making attainment of the vision possible. Jocelin's vision and Roger's calculation are required to create a spire and a novel. They complement one another as well as contrast with one another.

Pangall

This is true also of Pangall, parallel to Jocelin as scapegoat and lucky mascot, buried in the pit along with Jocelin's heads and his subconscious. They are linked by their connections with Goody, the one impotent, the other celibate. Both are builders or creators, but Pangall's cottage is a 'piecemeal construction', 'its random parts had slumped together' in contrast to Jocelin's original single, unified vision of the spire.

Goody

The other characters are also part of the pattern of the novel. Goody exists in Jocelin's imagination as a symbol of his sexual desires and fears, fusing in the 'uncountry' of his mind with the dumb man. Red hair, green cloak, occasional glimpse of white belly suggest the disembodied nature of his sexual fantasies. To him, she is both innocent child and bewitching devil. She remains as disembodied for the reader as for Jocelin.

Rachel

Rachel, whom Jocelin tries to ignore as much as possible, is, by contrast, given substance through dialogue, 'her whole body a part of speech'. Golding suggests the non-stop torrent of words by catching her in mid-sentence and then interspersing her continuous flow first with Jocelin's thoughts, then with snippets of conversation conducted across the babble. After this introduction to her, her speech patterns are merely suggested, mainly by repetition, and given in the third person. By this economical method, Golding makes us imagine the torrent of words without having to reproduce it. The outrageous red dress matches the outrageous account of her sex-life with Roger. Her sudden silence when Jocelin turns to face her after hearing Roger and Goody in the swallow's nest, shows that she has the sensitivity to read his expresision and to evoke a reciprocal response from him.

Other characters

The other characters are even more sketchy and the workmen are simply representative figures. In 'An Affection for Cathedrals' Golding says that looking at the gargoyles at Salisbury, 'you are looking straight at the life of seven hundred years ago, the life of tavern and street, the sweating, brawling, good-humoured life, (*A Moving Target*, 17).

Do you think the brief scenes in *The Spire* which suggest this 'sweating, brawling life' suffice to place the central story in such an imagined world? In this context, consider Jocelin's invitation to Roger to imagine what it is like to be a chisel. It is a wonderfully sympathetic account. Do you think

Golding has imposed excessive limitations on himself by making the centre of consciousness in the novel more able to imagine himself a chisel than another human being?

Whatever the answer to that question, we can say that the strength of the kind of novel Golding writes comes from the paring away of inessentials, while exploring complexities and multiple possibilities. In *The Spire* the contradictory qualities are achieved through Golding's use of Jocelin. In his speech of acceptance of the Nobel prize for literature, he said, 'There is no other medium in which we can live for so long and so intimately, with a character. That is the service a novel renders'.

5 SPECIMEN PASSAGE AND COMMENTARY

I have chosen this passage from Chapter 4 because it illustrates Golding's most powerful qualities as a novelist. I suggest you read it several times, noting the aspects of it which you find especially impressive, before looking at my comments.

'Look right at the bottom.'

He opened his eyes again, and the reflected sunlight in the pit was easy to them. It was peaceful, secluded. He could see the different kinds of soil all the way down. First there was stone, six inches of it, the slabs on which they knelt; then, as it were hanging from this lip, the sides became fragmented stone held together with accretions of lime. Beneath that again was a foot or two of furry things that might be the crushed and frayed ends of brushwood. Beneath that was dark earth, stuck everywhere with pebbles; and the bottom was a darker patch, with more pebbles. There seemed little enough to look at, but the quiet light from the metal sheet was restful; and no one made any noise.

Then, as Jocelin looked, he saw a pebble drop with two clods of earth; and immediately a patch perhaps a yard square fell out of the side below him and struck the bottom with a soft thud. The pebbles that fell with it lay shining dully in the reflected light, and settled themselves in their new bed. But as he watched them and waited for them to settle, the hair rose on the nape of his neck; for they never settled completely. He saw one stir, as with a sudden restlessness; and then he saw that they were all moving more or less, with a slow stirring, like the stirring of grubs. The earth was moving under the grubs, urging them this way and that, like porridge coming to the boil in a pot; and the grubs were made to crawl by it, as dust will crawl on the head of a tapped drum.

Jocelin jerked out his hand and made a defensive sign at the bottom of the pit. He glanced at Roger Mason, who was staring at the grubs, lips tight round his teeth, a yellow pallor shining through his skin which was not all reflection.

'What is it, Roger? What is it?'

Some form of life; that which ought not to be seen or touched, the darkness under the earth, turning, seething, coming to the boil.

'What is it? Tell me!'

But the master builder still strained down, eyes wide open.

Doomsday coming up. or the roof of hell down there. Perhaps the damned stirring, or the noseless men turning over and thrusting up; or the living, pagan earth, unbound at last and waking, Dia Mater. Jocelin found one hand coming up to his mouth; and all at once he was racked with spasms, and making the same sign over and over again.

There came a sharp scream from by the south west pillar. Goody Pangall stood there, her basket still rolling at her feet. From below the steps that led up to the wooden screen cutting off the choir, there came an imperious smack; and flicking or flinching that way, Jocelin saw bits of stone skittering out like pieces of smashed ice on the ice of a pond. One triangular piece the size of his palm slid to the edge of the pit and dropped in. And with the piece of stone, came something else; the high ringing of unbearable, unbelievable tension. It came from nowhere in particular, could not be placed, but sounded equally at the centre of things and at the periphery; it was needles in either ear. Another stone smacked down so that a leaping fragment clanged on the metal sheet.

All at once there was a tumult of human noises, shouts and curses and screams. There was movement too, which as it began, became at once violent and uncontrolled. There were many ways out of the crossways and no two people seemed to have the same idea about how to go. As he got to his feet and backed hastily away from the pit, Jocelin saw hands and faces, feet, hair, cloth and leather – saw them momentarily without taking them in. The metal screen went down with a crash. He was jerked against a pillar and a mouth – but whose mouth? – screamed near him.

'The earth's creeping!'

This passage shows Golding's skill in creating a process, succinctly and vividly. It starts with the human interchange – the invitation to look and Jocelin's tranquil looking. The sense of peaceful contemplation is established in three simple sentences. There follows a precise account of what is being contemplated; it might be a geologist's record of layers observed and identified. But the last sentence of this paragraph brings in again the human response; what Jocelin has seen seems 'little enough', the light is 'quiet', the metal sheet 'restful', 'and no one made any noise'.

Study this last phrase. Notice the simple sentence structure - subject, verb, object - the simple words - all except one are monosyllabic. Observe its position at the end of the paragraph, a little separated from the rest by the semi-colon. Its quiet, monosyllabic movement in itself creates a stillness, a pause, and so a sense of waiting for something.

The next sentence seems at first to fulfil that expectation. There is gradually increasing movement, first 'a pebble', then 'two clods' and then 'a patch a yard square' fall, and, for the first time sinceRoger spoke there is a sound, 'a dull thud'. Now Golding's skill in creating suspense becomes evident. All is peaceful again; the words are reassuring: the pebbles 'lay', their shine was 'dull', they 'settled' in a 'bed'. The tension is abruptly raised again by the switch to the subjective view. By telling us of Jocelin's horror - or rather, of the physical effect of his horror, the rising hair - he keeps his readers in appalled suspense about what is happening. Then he makes us see it, with a series of images whose impact is all the greater because the language has been so matter-of-face for most of the passage. But why do these images evoke such feelings of horror? Grubs are rather disgusting, perhaps, but there is nothing to appal in porridge or dust. But Golding has already created a state of suspense about any movement. Here, he uses repetition to heighten the menace: 'He saw one stir', 'all moving', 'a slow stirring, like the stirring of grubs'. Then the earth is moving, the grubs 'boil', the grubs 'crawl'. It is not only grubs but the whole earth relentlessly creeping; ordinary things like porridge and dust are caught up in the horror.

Jocelin's tense, nervous questions are the first sounds since the 'soft thud'. There is no answer to them. Neither Roger nor Jocelin can articulate their primeval fears. An unnamed voice speaks of 'some form of life'. The deliberate vagueness, like the negatives, 'ought not to be seen or touched' sets the imagination reeling. 'The darkness under the earth' implies a move into another dimension, beyond the explicable falling stones and moving mud.

The sharp, repeated questions evoke only mesmerised silence in response. Through deliberately vague and negative terms and unanswered questions, the giving of names to the experience is delayed. If Golding had started with Doomsday, hell and the damned, we would not have felt the evil so intensely. When he finally uses the traditional words, we do not see what they represent in a conventional or abstract way. He makes us have the experience first, and only afterwards labels it 'hell'. Even then, he is still working to prevent a detached or theoretical view of it. The damned, like the grubs, are 'stirring'. 'Noseless men . . . thrusting up', makes physical 'that which ought not to be seen', and the forceful verb, 'thrusting' suggests an aggressive, perhaps irresistible force. The reference to Dia Mater (she was the Greek moon-goddess of the oak-cult, thus linking up with the mistletoe and pagan workmen) brings the ancient religion, only partially suppressed, right into the foundations of the Christian church.

The methods used in the earlier paragraphs are repeated. Jocelin's mental state is indicated again through gesture. The absence of answers after the short, staccato questions intensifies the silence. The tension is screwed up to breaking-point. Abruptly, the 'sharp scream' shatters it, and all is movement and noise. Sound comes before seeing, 'an imperious smack' before Jocelin sees the cause of it. Then sight and sound work together to create that extraordinarily vivid image of 'smashed ice on the ice'. 'Flinching', 'flicking', 'skittering' suggest the quick, sharp movements; then the phrase, 'one triangular piece the size of his palm' slows everything down while we register size and shape (not movement). The diverse noises and movements are stilled as the stone simply 'slid to the edge of the pit and dropped in'. The monosyllabic words convey a quietness before the transition to a new kind of noise, which seems to grow out of the quietness. This unbearable, cosmic sound 'at the centre of things and at the periphery' heightens the tension again, until it is broken by the clang of stone on metal.

This paragraph is a superb piece of prose. Try reading it aloud, noticing the effects of the sounds and the rhythms of the sentences. Observe the techniques used to make you hear and see. In Chapter 4 of this book, I commented adversely on some of the ways in which Golding uses onomatopoeia. Here it fulfils its function perfectly. Words are chosen for their sounds, but there is no attempt to represent pure sound with meaningless syllables. The effect is taut, concentrated, vivid.

With the clang on the metal, the tension shatters in a jumble of human noises and movements replacing the sharp, hard sounds of stone, metal and ice and the piercing ringing. Golding suggests the chaos by listing fragments of human beings – hands, faces, a screaming mouth. Even the sentence structure, by its fragmentation – 'a mouth – but whose mouth? – screamed' – contributes to the sense of disintegration.

The precision of the detail makes reading this passage a gripping sensuous experience. We feel we are there, staring into the pit, noticing every pebble. The narrative skill in creating the actuality and the suspense is characteristic of the whole novel, but in passages of heightened tension like this one, the interplay of the different levels of meaning is conveyed in an especially powerful way. The sheer physical experience is immensely important. This is why Jocelin's own fear is conveyed through gesture rather than by describing his feelings.

The imagery keeps us in touch – just – with the ordinary world of cooking porridge, tapping a drum, watching ice 'skittering' on a pond. Because of these images, we know we are not in a fantasy world. This is here and now. While these images keep us in touch with the world recognised by our conscious minds, the pit images what is hidden, inexplicable, uncontrollable.

How close to us, as twentieth-century readers, is this seething hellmouth? Henry James, in the preface to *The Turn of the Screw* said 'Only make the reader's vision of evil intense enough . . . Make him *think* the evil, make him think it for himself'. Golding does this by making us see and hear with such intensity that our imagination is stimulated to create terrors beyond what we can see and hear. He has tapped that terror of the unknown which for medieval people was expressed in terms of hell and which for us is the awareness of things repressed in the human psyche but capable of 'thrusting up' in moments of crisis such as the one here, which leads to the murder of Pangall and in any period leads to wars, killing, torture.

In the context of the whole novel, this passage is an image of these unknown forces. The pit, dug by a builder in the course of his work, gives a physical form to repressed fears and desires. The frantic filling-in of the pit which follows this extract is a graphic illustration of repression. For a few appalling moments human beings had stared 'eyes wide open' at their deepest fears. Then they quickly buried what they saw.

This is central to Golding's conception of what the novel is for. His novels endeavour to sustain that wide open stare. He wrote, 'What man *is* . . . that I burn to know and that – I do not say this lightly – I would endure knowing.' (*A Moving Target*, 199).

6 CRITICAL RECEPTION

The immediate response to the publication of *The Spire* in April 1964 ranged from highly favourable, through somewhat guarded, to violently antagonistic. A surprising number of reviewers stated confidently that the spire fell at the end – the result, presumably of hasty reading for review purposes. As he wrote of its collapse, John Wain referred to 'practised readers of Golding who know what to expect'. Having expectations certainly coloured some responses. Wain described the novel as having Golding's usual limitations: 'writing to a preconceived thesis, neatly fashioned symbolic material, an excess of allegory'. It sounds more like a description of *Pincher Martin*. However, he also praised it for its other typical qualities, especially the 'power of creating excitement'.

Those critics who saw that Golding was doing something new in *The Spire* usually appreciated it more and were more perceptive about it than those who assumed it was a repetition of previous themes and methods. Ian Gregor emphasised the difference from the earlier novels: 'the line between good and evil is more obliquely drawn', 'the characters face now one way, now another'. *The Times Literary Supplement* saw the strength of the book 'not in its moral substance but in the way the meaning emerges naturally from the mythic material'. Nevertheless, it also pointed out that 'Golding has moralistic designs on us' and stressed that 'he isolates what is basic and avoids the merely contemporary, social, subjective'. It saw the spire as 'a magnificent symbol' but everything else as weak in comparison. P. N. Furbank and Ian Gregor combined very high praise of the novel with similar comments on weaknesses in handling human relationships, especially sexual ones. Goody was felt to be inadequate and Furbank thought that Jocelin's lust for her 'never comes to life'. But he called the novel 'a splendid success' and commented especially on the visual power of the writing – 'You live with this building operation' – and the strength of the prose, especially at crisis points. This was in contrast to several reviewers who found it overwritten, obscure or just inadequate – 'his intentions are honourable but words fail him' (Francis Wyndham).

Ian Gregor described *The Spire* as 'a great "dare" coming off finely' and the reviewer in *The Times Literary Supplement* and P. N. Furbank in *Encounter* took similar views.

V. S. Pritchett made its difference from the earlier novels the main basis for a violent attack, in an article which ends, 'As a humanist Golding is a good novelist; as a symbolist or a mystic, he fails – especially as a mystic. Better get back to humanism – and other people'. The main line of his argument is that the book is merely a vehicle for 'that self-indulgent provider of rhetoric, and diatribe, the excited author'. He complains that 'we are muddled about the meaning of it all, we suspect the author of believing that chaos heightens poetic insight'.

This variety of reactions to *The Spire* makes Frank McGuiness's onslaught in the *London Magazine* rather surprising. He delayed his review until August 1964, in order to be able to attack 'the magazine pundits' who see Golding's work as inviting 'not so much criticism as genuflecting, if frequently perplexed, tribute to the revealed word'. He maintained that what it is about is 'largely a matter of guesswork' owing to the 'mannered incoherence' of the style. He ended on a flippant note; 'Jocelin's spire . . . is like some gigantic phallus reminding us of the vileness of our nature. It's a thought. The pity is that the author could not have made it less dull, strained and monotonous'.

Frank Kermode's essay was first written in 1964 and republished in his collection of essays, *Continuities* in 1968. For him, it demonstrates how Golding writes 'each new novel as if he had written no other'. He comments on the density and fierceness of language, and the power to 'generate meanings which grow out of the fiction and are not imposed on it'. It is about 'vision and its cost', but this summing-up is inadequate because the whole work is 'a dance of figurative language' requiring unremitting attention. It is also 'as much about Golding writing a novel as anything else'. He concludes: 'It is remote from the mainstream, potent, severe, even forbidding. And in its way a marvel'.

The chapter on *The Spire* in *William Golding* (1967) by Kinkead-Weekes and Gregor develops some of the points made by Gregor in his 1964 *Guardian* article. The notion of duality is explored more fully. They show Golding setting a series of patterns at war and showing that none will do. They also elaborate on the 'novel about writing a novel' theme. This is a detailed and illuminating study of the book.

Also in 1967 D. W. Crompton's essay was published in the *Critical Quarterly* (an enlarged version can be found in his *The View from The Spire* (1985)). This is perhaps the most interesting of the 'source-hunting' essays, of which there are many. Crompton draws parallels with T. S. Eliot's

The Wasteland, Browning's 'The Bishop orders his Tomb', Ibsen's *The Master Builder*, and, most fruitfully, the Norse myth of Balder.

Arnold Johnston's *Of Earth and Darkness* (1980) takes the unusual view that in this novel Golding examines wide ranges of human relationships, a coherent social fabric and the rhythms of social change. Jocelin's story is 'part of a larger sociocultural process' leading to the Renaissance. While Johnston's main stress is on 'the intensity of its central drama' he also claims that the novel 'undeniably captures the flavour of the period and its sense of sociocultural turmoil'.

One of the most interesting considerations of Golding comes in Gabriel Josipovici's *The World and the Book* (1971), an examination of a number of books ranging in time from the Middle Ages to the present. He places *The Spire* in relation to the earlier novels, saying that it is here that Golding, fortunately, 'pulls back from the desire to explain'. He comments on the 'steel-like quality which makes one feel that every superfluous flourish has been removed'; 'the overall shape of a Golding novel is what is interesting about it. He then develops in a particularly interesting way the parallel between Jocelin's will, pushing up the spire 'foot by foot', and the author's will, moving the novel forward 'page by page'. He sees the act of reading, too, as part of the process, 'we grow dizzy from this height . . . perhaps it is only we who hold up this ediface'. Josipovici points out that unlike Pincher's rock, the spire is still there at the end: 'It has become public property since it is made out of public things: words, wood, stones'. He ends by pointing to the effort of imagination needed to accept this product – *The Spire*. 'Such an effort this book can teach us to make.'

QUESTIONS

1. 'I think it is true to say of my books that the needle tends to quiver over towards ideas rather than towards people . . . I would put it down as the basic defect of my books.' Consider, with reference to *The Spire*, whether you agree with Golding's assessment of his fiction.

2. In 'A Moving Target', Golding asks, 'Why did I not choose the gasworks [chimney]? . . . More than that, is the novel that eventuated about the spire at all?' What answers to Golding's questions would you suggest?

3. A contemporary novelist writes of the search for 'possible ways in which we who are writing now will be able to express our sense of evil'. Does *The Spire* offer ways in which we who are reading now are able to experience a sense of evil?

4. 'A fierce concentrated light plays on a restricted area' (Golding). Is this simultaneously a source of strength and weakness in *The Spire*?

5. Examine some of the methods Golding uses to make 'you feel as if you've helped build the spire'.

6. 'I tried to draw a few simple lines on the sky' (Jocelin). Do you think *The Spire* also simplifes?

7. Golding considers that 'the bad side of mankind is more accessible to the novelist'. Do you think he has simply gone for what is easy in *The Spire*?

8. Is it a limitation of *The Spire* that the sense of transcendent good and evil is not wedded to a fully-felt social novel?

9. How would you answer the critic who asked, 'Hasn't Golding misused the form he is working with? Shouldn't we regard the books as tracts?'

10. 'There is no other medium in which we can live for so long and so intimately with a character. That is the service a novel renders' Golding's speech in acceptance of the Nobel Prize for Literature). What methods has Golding used to achieve this in *The Spire*?

FURTHER READING

Recommended text
Golding, William, *The Spire* (London: Faber & Faber, 1964).

Other novels by Golding
Lord of the Flies (London: Faber & Faber, 1954).
The Inheritors (London: Faber & Faber, 1955).
Pincher Martin (London: Faber & Faber, 1956).
Darkness Visible (London: Faber & Faber, 1979).

Essays by Golding
The Hot Gates, and other occasional pieces (London: Faber & Faber, 1965)
   ('Fable'; 'Egypt from my Inside'; 'The Ladder and the Tree').
A Moving Target (London: Faber & Faber, 1982) ('An Affection for
   Cathedrals'; 'Rough Magic'; 'A Moving Target'; 'Belief and Creativity').

Works by other authors
Kinkead-Weeks, M. and Gregor, I. *William Golding* (London: Faber &
   Faber, 1984) revised edn.
Josipovici, G., *The World and the Book* (London: Macmillan, 1971)
   chap. 10, but also chaps 11 and 12.
Kermode, F., *Continuities* (London: Routledge & Kegan Paul, 1968).

Also from Macmillan

CASEBOOK SERIES

The Macmillan *Casebook* series brings together the best of modern criticism with a selection of early reviews and comments. Each Casebook charts the development of opinion on a play, poem, or novel, or on a literary genre, from its first appearance to the present day.

GENERAL THEMES

COMEDY: DEVELOPMENTS IN CRITICISM
D. J. Palmer

DRAMA CRITICISM: DEVELOPMENTS SINCE IBSEN
A. J. Hinchliffe

THE ENGLISH NOVEL: DEVELOPMENTS IN CRITICISM SINCE HENRY JAMES
Stephen Hazell

THE LANGUAGE OF LITERATURE
N. Page

THE PASTORAL MODE
Bryan Loughrey

THE ROMANTIC IMAGINATION
J. S. Hill

TRAGEDY: DEVELOPMENTS IN CRITICISM
R. P. Draper

POETRY

WILLIAM BLAKE: SONGS OF INNOCENCE AND EXPERIENCE
Margaret Bottrall

BROWNING: MEN AND WOMEN AND OTHER POEMS
J. R. Watson

BYRON: CHILDE HAROLD'S PILGRIMAGE AND DON JUAN
John Jump

CHAUCER: THE CANTERBURY TALES
J. J. Anderson

COLERIDGE: THE ANCIENT MARINER AND OTHER POEMS
A. R. Jones and W. Tydeman

DONNE: SONGS AND SONETS
Julian Lovelock

T. S. ELIOT: FOUR QUARTETS
Bernard Bergonzi

T. S. ELIOT: PRUFROCK, GERONTION, ASH WEDNESDAY AND OTHER POEMS
B. C. Southam

T. S. ELIOT: THE WASTELAND
C. B. Cox and A. J. Hinchliffe

ELIZABETHAN POETRY: LYRICAL AND NARRATIVE
Gerald Hammond

THOMAS HARDY: POEMS
J. Gibson and T. Johnson

GERALD MANLEY HOPKINS: POEMS
Margaret Bottrall

KEATS: ODES
G. S. Fraser

KEATS: THE NARRATIVE POEMS
J. S. Hill

MARVELL: POEMS
Arthur Pollard

THE METAPHYSICAL POETS
Gerald Hammond

MILTON: PARADISE LOST
A. E. Dyson and Julian Lovelock

POETRY OF THE FIRST WORLD WAR
Dominic Hibberd

ALEXANDER POPE: THE RAPE OF THE LOCK
John Dixon Hunt

SHELLEY: SHORTER POEMS & LYRICS
Patrick Swinden

SPENSER: THE FAERIE QUEEN
Peter Bayley

TENNYSON: IN MEMORIAM
John Dixon Hunt

THIRTIES POETS: 'THE AUDEN GROUP'
Ronald Carter

WORDSWORTH: LYRICAL BALLADS
A. R. Jones and W. Tydeman

WORDSWORTH: THE PRELUDE
W. J. Harvey and R. Gravil

W. B. YEATS: POEMS 1919–1935
E. Cullingford

W. B. YEATS: LAST POEMS
Jon Stallworthy

THE NOVEL AND PROSE

JANE AUSTEN: EMMA
David Lodge

JANE AUSTEN: NORTHANGER ABBEY AND PERSUASION
B. C. Southam

JANE AUSTEN: SENSE AND SENSIBILITY, PRIDE AND PREJUDICE AND MANSFIELD PARK
B. C. Southam

CHARLOTTE BRONTË: JANE EYRE AND VILLETTE
Miriam Allott

EMILY BRONTË: WUTHERING HEIGHTS
Miriam Allott

BUNYAN: THE PILGRIM'S PROGRESS
R. Sharrock

CONRAD: HEART OF DARKNESS, NOSTROMO AND UNDER WESTERN EYES
C. B. Cox

CONRAD: THE SECRET AGENT
Ian Watt

CHARLES DICKENS: BLEAK HOUSE
A. E. Dyson

CHARLES DICKENS: DOMBEY AND SON AND LITTLE DORRITT
Alan Shelston

CHARLES DICKENS: HARD TIMES, GREAT EXPECTATIONS AND OUR MUTUAL FRIEND
N. Page

GEORGE ELIOT: MIDDLEMARCH
Patrick Swinden

GEORGE ELIOT: THE MILL ON THE FLOSS AND SILAS MARNER
R. P. Draper

HENRY FIELDING: TOM JONES
Neil Compton

E. M. FORSTER: A PASSAGE TO INDIA
Malcolm Bradbury

HARDY: THE TRAGIC NOVELS
R. P. Draper

HENRY JAMES: WASHINGTON SQUARE AND THE PORTRAIT OF A LADY
Alan Shelston

JAMES JOYCE: DUBLINERS AND A PORTRAIT OF THE ARTIST AS A YOUNG MAN
Morris Beja

D. H. LAWRENCE: THE RAINBOW AND WOMEN IN LOVE
Colin Clarke

D. H. LAWRENCE: SONS AND LOVERS
Gamini Salgado

SWIFT: GULLIVER'S TRAVELS
Richard Gravil

THACKERAY: VANITY FAIR
Arthur Pollard

TROLLOPE: THE BARSETSHIRE
NOVELS
T. Bareham

VIRGINIA WOOLF: TO THE
LIGHTHOUSE
Morris Beja

DRAMA

CONGREVE: COMEDIES
Patrick Lyons

T. S. ELIOT: PLAYS
Arnold P. Hinchliffe

JONSON: EVERY MAN IN HIS
HUMOUR AND THE ALCHEMIST
R. V. Holdsworth

JONSON: VOLPONE
J. A. Barish

MARLOWE: DR FAUSTUS
John Jump

MARLOWE: TAMBURLAINE,
EDWARD II AND THE JEW OF
MALTA
John Russell Brown

MEDIEVAL ENGLISH DRAMA
Peter Happé

O'CASEY: JUNO AND THE
PAYCOCK, THE PLOUGH AND THE
STARS AND THE SHADOW OF A
GUNMAN
R. Ayling

JOHN OSBORNE: LOOK BACK IN
ANGER
John Russell Taylor

WEBSTER: THE WHITE DEVIL AND
THE DUCHESS OF MALFI
R. V. Holdsworth

WILDE: COMEDIES
W. Tydeman

SHAKESPEARE

SHAKESPEARE: ANTONY AND
CLEOPATRA
John Russell Brown

SHAKESPEARE: CORIOLANUS
B. A. Brockman

SHAKESPEARE: HAMLET
John Jump

SHAKESPEARE: HENRY IV PARTS
I AND II
G. K. Hunter

SHAKESPEARE: HENRY V
Michael Quinn

SHAKESPEARE: JULIUS CAESAR
Peter Ure

SHAKESPEARE: KING LEAR
Frank Kermode

SHAKESPEARE: MACBETH
John Wain

SHAKESPEARE: MEASURE FOR
MEASURE
G. K. Stead

SHAKESPEARE: THE MERCHANT
OF VENICE
John Wilders

SHAKESPEARE: A MIDSUMMER
NIGHT'S DREAM
A. W. Price

SHAKESPEARE: MUCH ADO
ABOUT NOTHING AND AS YOU
LIKE IT
John Russell Brown

SHAKESPEARE: OTHELLO
John Wain

SHAKESPEARE: RICHARD II
N. Brooke

SHAKESPEARE: THE SONNETS
Peter Jones

SHAKESPEARE: THE TEMPEST
D. J. Palmer

SHAKESPEARE: TROILUS AND
CRESSIDA
Priscilla Martin

SHAKESPEARE: TWELFTH NIGHT
D. J. Palmer

SHAKESPEARE: THE WINTER'S
TALE
Kenneth Muir

Mastering English Literature

Richard Gill

Mastering English Literature will help readers both to enjoy English Literature and to be successful in 'O' levels, 'A' levels and other public exams. It is an introduction to the study of poetry, novels and drama which helps the reader in four ways – by providing ways of approaching literature, by giving examples and practice exercises, by offering hints on how to write about literature, and by the author's own evident enthusiasm for the subject. With extracts from more than 200 texts, this is an enjoyable account of how to get the maximum satisfaction out of reading, whether it be for formal examinations or simply for pleasure.

Work Out English Literature ('A' level)

S.H. Burton

This book familiarises 'A' level English Literature candidates with every kind of test which they are likely to encounter. Suggested answers are worked out step by step and accompanied by full author's commentary. The book helps students to clarify their aims and establish techniques and standards so that they can make appropriate responses to similar questions when the examination pressures are on. It opens up fresh ways of looking at the full range of set texts, authors and critical judgements and motivates students to know more of these matters.

Also published by Macmillan

Mastering English Language S. H. Burton
Mastering English Grammar S. H. Burton
Workout English Language ('O' level and GCSE) S. H. Burton